WORDS FROM THE HEDGE

# WORDS FROM THE HEDGE

A Hedgelayer's View of the Countryside

Richard Negus

unbound

First published in 2025

Unbound
An imprint of Boundless Publishing Group
c/o Max Accountants, Ketton Suite, The King Centre,
Main Road, Barleythorpe, Rutland, LE15 7WD
www.unbound.com
All rights reserved

© Richard Negus, 2025

Foreword © John Lewis-Stempel, 2025
Internal illustrations © Becca Thorne, 2025

The right of Richard Negus to be identified as the author of this work has been asserted in accordance with Section 77 of the Copyright, Designs and Patents Act, 1988. No part of this publication may be copied, reproduced, stored in a retrieval system, or transmitted, in any form or by any means without the prior permission of the publisher, nor be otherwise circulated in any form of binding or cover other than that in which it is published and without a similar condition being imposed on the subsequent purchaser.

Typeset by Jouve (UK), Milton Keynes

A CIP record for this book is available from the British Library

ISBN 978-1-78965-203-1 (hardback)
ISBN 978-1-78965-204-8 (ebook)

Printed in Great Britain by Clays Ltd, Elcograf S.p.A.

1 3 5 7 9 8 6 4 2

To Clare, my world.

Contents

Foreword	ix
Prologue	1
1 *Terroir*, the country I know	17
2 Practical Conservationists	28
3 Plan then Plant	45
4 Silent Jim	60
5 Flea Barn	74
6 Bucolic	99
7 Deadly Darren	119
8 Flailing About	138
9 Enemies?	157
10 Regrowth	178
Conservation hedgelaying and how you can do it	193
Some favoured plants for an East Anglian hedge	195
A Note on Sources	201
Acknowledgements	203
Supporters	205
A Note on the Author	211
A Note on the Type	213

Foreword

IF YOU TOOK A billhook to the soul of Britain, you'd find a hedge growing there. A good country hedge is an instant emblem of these isles, as much as Stonehenge, an oak tree in a meadow, or a downland chalk stream. Exiled in Berlin, the poet Rupert Brooke dreamed of home where 'Unkempt about those hedges blows / An English unofficial rose'; upon reaching Britain from hedge-bare continental Europe, the poet Elizabeth Barrett Browning was delighted to re-encounter a land where 'All the fields / Are tied up fast with hedges, nosegay-like.'

Why does the hedge resonate so much? Brooke and Barrett Browning doubtless recognised in the hedge a form of craft, even an art. A hedge is human-made, a living sculpture formed by many hands over timeless years. In the past, men and women literally went to war to protect the British countryside, partly for its beauty, but partly because they recognised the hedged landscape as their heritage, a place characterised by the handiwork of their forefathers and foremothers. The Great British hedge stretches back to prehistoric times. The maintenance of a hedge is the preservation of agriculture.

Now we are at the thorny matter. Ironically, our hedges have no place in either industrialised food production or 'rewilding', since both eschew human care for the countryside. (A hedge would be swallowed up by the wolfy wildwood of a Britain returned to 3000 BC). But the hedge is the farmer's true friend – it is stock fence, windbreak, defence against erosion, medicine chest for ill livestock (you let them browse to self-medicate). Apart from its agricultural virtues, a good hedge is a nature reserve, a home for fauna and flora. Some of the best habitats for nature are actually human-made. I know it seems impossible to say such a thing these days when rewilding sucks up the conservation movement's oxygen, but it is true. Think of a traditional hay meadow. Or a pond. Or, of course, a hedge.

Richard Negus is a proper conservationist; he knows his stuff, because he does the stuff. He is a master hedger, a hands-on man with, as we say in the country, 'a head on him'. He's a thinker, and he can lay, bind and prune his wise words with consummate skill. His pen and his eyes are as sharp as his bill-hook. Like Gilbert White, BB (Denys Watkins-Pitchford) and other great rural writers, he gives you the view of the country-side from the inside out, and up personal and close. He also happens to know a collection of can-do conservationists and real East Anglian country people who, frankly, are a threatened species themselves.

A hedge is a leafy line of beauty, heritage and utility. It is a habitat too. Richard Negus shows us the wondrous life of the hedge, but above all how hedges, and the philosophy of the human-nature partnership that they embody, can mend the countryside. Hedges are the way ahead. And in Richard Negus they have their one true champion.

John Lewis-Stempel
April 2023

Prologue

My chainsaw requires an elaborate series of pumping, priming and lever-twisting. Only then, followed by repeated pulls on its cord, can I coax the engine into spluttering life. It hates me stopping for a tea break. It's a machine that came out of a factory in Germany, but it seems to have moods and foibles. Cold weather makes it race; warm weather makes it reluctant. A fifteen-minute rest leaves it like a dozing soldier, reluctant to perform its duties. I turn back to the hedge, glancing at the stems I cut and laid before I stopped to sip a cup of sweet black tea, scalding hot from my battered flask. They lie one over the next like a thorny row of toppled dominoes. Long scars stare out where I have chopped through the stems – or pleachers, as they are called in our strange language of the hedge. So pale when first cut, they have now started to change colour. The maple turns orange, the spindle ivory-like, and the hazel and hawthorn turn cookie brown. I make some upward cuts with my saw, taking away the side growth from a hawthorn pleacher. It is January and there are no leaves on this gnarled limb, and only a handful of berries, unclaimed by the blackbirds and thrushes, still cling on.

I bend to cut my clean, straight pleacher now it is cleared of encumbrances. The little saw roars once more and I make a diagonal cut downwards from right to left. I watch with an attentive eye through the mesh of my safety visor, looking for the base of the thorn to give slightly. This indicates I have made my cut sufficiently deep and reduces the rigidity of the growing plant. The top of my wrist flips the saw's safety bar forward and my thumb depresses the stop button.

The shift from anarchic roar to silence is dizzying. Yet there is never real silence here. Rooks caw persistently, and the chittering and squabbling of long-tailed tits is endless. One of the cock pheasants crows a challenge over at the wood some two fields away. He quits his row and I hear him ruffle his mantle when he hears no rival's reply. Placing my saw down to my right, with gloved hands I bend the thorny pleacher gently over. Using my billhook to make a final cut, I lay the clean limb to nestle and intertwine with its neighbour. The hinge does its job. Thick enough to support the pleacher in its new position of forty degrees or so, but sufficiently flexible to allow me to alter nature. I flick the chainsaw back into life. Warmed up now, it is speedily responsive. I trim off the heel of the stool – the term for the still-living root-stock – and take a sideways step to my right to repeat the process with the next branch, then the next, then the next. I will stake and bind my hedge before the sun starts to go down; this will guard my work from the wind that loves to pluck at a hedge and undo hours of labour. When I drive away, I survey the thorny line in the gleam of my truck's headlights. It is a sight I never grow tired of, and it pays my bills.

The stylised image of a hedgelayer is that of a pipe-smoking rustic, cutting away in a towering line of thorn and branch with a viciously sharp, curiously shaped billhook. This ancient tool was first used to trim Assyrian vines and briars; bronze examples, thought to be over 1,000 years old, have been found in Egypt. Over time, the billhook lost its role as a tool of regeneration and was instead called upon to become a thing of destruction. It could slice through muscle, bone and sinew, the makeshift weapon of serfs and bondsmen dragooned into leaving land-based toil to become soldiers.

I own three billhooks. The youngest, a Yorkshire-style hook, was made in 1941, and is stamped with a military crow's foot. Another is a spar hook, the blade thinner and longer, made and still used for cleaving hazel to make spars for thatching. My oldest, and favourite – a Midland-style bill – was crafted by a long-forgotten Leicestershire smith in the 1920s. Curiously, it is made in a Devonshire pattern, yet I doubt the man who made it had ever ventured out of his county, let alone made the long trek to the South West. As the decades have rolled by, its handle has been replaced numerous times, but the cutting blade still takes an edge as only old hand-forged steel can. I was told once by an agricultural engineer that steel made prior to the atomic-bomb drops on Hiroshima and Nagasaki is superior to everything that came after. Radionuclide contamination, he said, and I believed him. A few purists sneer at my using a chainsaw to lay hedges, claiming that an axe should be used if a pleacher is too thick to be cut with a billhook. Many of these idealists are amateurs, extremely talented amateurs it must be said, competing in hedgelaying competitions throughout the land (and working in warm offices during the week while I'm out in the rain). But I have a job to do and I'm on the clock. The niceties and purities of craft are as relevant to me as a traction engine is to the tractor driver discing a field in his behemoth John Deere. I have a mile of hedge to lay and I don't have time to dwell upon tradition for the sake of tradition.

Hedges, unlike some woodland, are and always will be a construct of man. Romano Britons cut and laid small trees to form livestock retaining enclosures. Gaps were filled by transplanting thorny shrubs; these saplings were protected with cut brash. The traces of these early hedges can still be seen today. After harvest, when the summer sun bakes the stubbles dusty yellow, the land reveals ancient secrets to the questing camera of the drone. Dark lines, the memories of hedgerows long gone, spread out like the veins on the back of an old man's hand. As crop production increased, so hedges proliferated; they kept browsing wildlife out and gifted tender plants protection from the elements. Hedges acted as almost permanent boundaries; their permanency led to the fields being given names. What would Sheffield, Huddersfield or Enfield be without the hedge? Hedges became walls, delineating the ownership of land. When hedges grew too large and shaded out growing crops they were cut. If gaps appeared, enabling cattle or sheep to escape, they were filled by laid lengths. When the hedges got in the way they were coppiced and hacked. But these hedgerow battlements were too massive by now to be removed by mere hand tools. Trees were left behind and grew from sapling into elm or curlicued oak. The blackthorn suckers merely waited for a back to be turned to spring up and become a bank of scrub. These ancients had no thought, I suspect, that their hedgerow planting and management was providing habitat for wildlife. The hedge for them was a tool, a manageable means of ensuring their livestock received shelter and stayed in the place it was supposed to be. The idea that our forebears were somehow totally at one with nature seems a little romantic. More mundanely, the early farmers twigged that the hedge was simply yet another example of natural phenomena that they could harness and then master for their own ends.

Hedgerow plants such as hawthorn, blackthorn, field maple, hazel, dogwood and rose all happily grow in fruit-bowl-jumbled profusion in hedgerows, jostling with one another for dominance. The hedge apes, in human-made linear form, naturally occurring scrub. Scrub plants are the secondary species found in woodland, the nursemaids of lowland England's great primary trees – oak, ash, elm, beech and hornbeam. Hedge shrubs are precocious, sufficiently forgiving to allow man to cut and trim them to his whim, yet growing and regrowing with a speed, density and thickness that suits our needs. It was mere coincidence that man's creation of the hedge suited wildlife.

A mixed hedge plays home to prolific nature. Tree and house sparrows, yellowhammers, linnets, robins, blackbirds, thrushes, wrens, tits both blue and great and finches – be they green, chaf, gold or bull – rear their young in the cross-work of limbs. The grey partridge and pheasant escape from raptors in its thorny understory and weave their ground nests in the hedgerow's lee. Shrews, mice and voles scurry and feed here. The hedgehog's very name denotes its preferred habitat, although in hedge-light early-mediaeval England the hedgehog was known as an *urchin* – prickly yet edible. Rabbits and rats tunnel amongst the roots; the stoats and weasels follow, hunting them. Deer shelter from the elements here and badgers build their cavernous setts; foxes take up residence when brock decides to evacuate. Invertebrates – beetles, aphids, bees, flies, wasps and mites – call the hedge home. All-comers feast upon the fruit borne by the hedge in autumn. This man-made haven, created to keep cows and sheep in and wind and rain out, is so much more than a barrier. If the woods are the lungs of the land, the hedgerows are its arteries.

In Britain we have had a good number of revolutions. One regicidal, one industrial and the rest agricultural. In the eighteenth century, while France clamoured for *liberté, égalité et fraternité*, we rebelled via enclosure and the four-field rotation system. Our men of change were Jethro Tull, 'Farmer' George III and Robert Bakewell. Open-field, or strip, farming was in rapid decline by the early 1700s. The invention of the horse-drawn seed drill meant that crops could be sown in straight lines. Straight lines were previously unheard of in the agrarian landscape – there is no such thing as plumb linear in nature. These arrow path drills meant that a horse-drawn hoe could be used to suppress weeds. Landowners no longer needed to make their money via rents paid by a multitude of strip-farming husbandmen. Instead, they could enclose their lands and farm for themselves. Some husbandmen became paid employees of their erstwhile landlords. Many more turned their back on the land and headed to the smoke and cinders of the emerging industrial conurbations. The hedge became a barrier of a different nature, keeping out the wandering house cow or the litter of pigs owned by the landless. Common land became less common. The hedge was both an image of the ending of old freedoms and simultaneously a totem of improvement. In France, the symbol of revolution was the guillotine. In rural England it was the hedge.

I have a copy of the Ordnance Survey map of Suffolk for 1881. Nearly two centuries after Jethro Tull's horse-drawn hoe first made its appearance, the land shown is still a patchwork of small fields. The sheer number of individual farms speaks of times when a large farmer was someone with a hundred acres rather than thousands of hectares. Countless farms are surrounded by a spider's web of lines marking the hedgerows. Most of the fields are all odd angles and awkward corners. No problem for a ploughman and a team of Suffolk Punch horses to deal with, but a cash-sapping disaster of stopping, starting and turning for modern machinery. Each land parcel is of a similar size. Hedges are dotted with standard trees, intricately marked by the draughtsman's pen nib. Doubtless most, if not all, of the hedgerow trees would have had their limbs pollarded, reducing field shade and providing the timber used for fuel – in East Anglia, where coal was the preserve of the rich, food was cooked and houses were warmed by wood fires. While nearly all of the hedgerows inked on this map are long gone, a hardy few remain. These living marks of times past, the maple and hawthorn, elm sucker and blackthorn, hazel and dog rose, are the offspring of Victorian hedges. In turn, those nineteenth-century barriers were borne by hedges dating back to the Enclosures Act. The word Act should in truth be pluralised. Between 1604 and 1914 over 5,000 individual Acts were put in place, enclosing nearly 7 million acres, ridding the landscape of subsistence landholdings to create consolidated and profitable farms. Open-field farming was dead and the hedge had taken root across the countryside.

This was a landscape that remained more or less unchanged until 1914. It was on 28 June that year when the Bosnian Serb Gavrilo Princip succeeded in shooting both Archduke Ferdinand and his wife the Duchess of Hohenberg. His marksmanship cost the countryside much. Farm labourers, gamekeepers and estate workers flocked to the colours. Their employers were also commissioned with rapidity. Off they went to the mire and blood of Flanders or the Dardanelles, many never to return. While Tommies died in their tens of thousands, arguably the truly 'lost generation' of the Great War was the officer corps. The life expectancy of a subaltern on the Western Front was a mere six weeks. With few heirs to carry on estates, a crash in agricultural income, the introduction of death duties and sweeping tax hikes spelled the end of the old ways. A shift in land ownership now occurred; nearly one quarter of farmland in England and Wales changed hands between 1918 and 1927. The new lords of the manor were a different animal from their predecessors. The old squirearchy in all their stuffy, minor-aristocratic ways had been loath to change much; hedges were valuable to their shooting interests, as were the woods. A lack of ready cash meant that mechanisation of agriculture had been slow to take hold. The new landlords, however, were men of action and commerce. Many were from the stock who had fled the land to join the Industrial Revolution in the eighteenth and nineteenth centuries. These men had made their money in the town and had now returned to bring their business brains to the land.

It would be wrong to say that the countryside changed overnight following the end of the Great War. A few bright young things spurned Baden Powell's Scouts, who were perceived as too militaristic and rigid. They joined instead the ranks of the quasi-spiritual, proto-environmentalist Kindred of the Kibbo

Kift, the Woodcraft Folk or the Green Shirts – an early twentieth-century equivalent to Extinction Rebellion but with less angry protest and more camping and folk dancing. The big-bag Edwardian shooting squire had also evolved. Sickened by the mass slaughter he had seen in France, he shunned 'big bags', turning to a more a considered approach, cherishing the wild game that inhabited his acres, heralding the dawn of the Game Conservancy. The countryside became seen as something pure, honest and clean, certainly when compared with the corruption of the trenches or the fire and brimstone of the industrial towns. Naturalists including the writer Henry Williamson, the folklorist Rolf Gardiner, and agriculturalists such as Jorian Jenks melded together their English proto-organicism, love of wildlife and delight in farming, advocating a troubling political philosophy of blood and soil.

The German invasion of Poland in 1939 put paid to peace in Britain. And the brave new world of 1945 was markedly different from that of 1918. We began to lose meadows, wetlands, trees and hedges after the Second World War. The word *lost* is too genteel: they were destroyed, smashed and erased – by saw and plough, by digger and dynamite. But this was no act of vandalism led by those who had bought land after the First World War. It was driven by government diktat. The nation was hungry and desiccated. Brought down by a cash-sapping, man-grinding war against totalitarianism. Victory in Europe brought to the British countryside a brutal modernism. The science and technology that had been used so successfully to kill off the cults of Nazism, Fascism and Japanese imperialism were turned to the land. The new pesticides and herbicides that were being introduced had been developed as chemical weapons of war. The munitions that levelled Dresden and Hamburg were re-employed to explode ancient elms and towering oaks, turning them to smouldering rootless splinters. And machinery that had stormed the beaches of Normandy was adapted then enlisted to erase hedges. The land now had one job to do – feed the nation. Farmland that had been a partnership, albeit a fairly one-sided one, between man and wildlife, shifted to become a human dictatorship. Every square yard needed to be productive. Woodland and wetland, trees and hedges, were enemies of mass production. The small land parcels seen in the map of 1881 were wasteful; they hampered the new, ever-larger, brutal agricultural machinery in reaping their economical monoculture harvests. If England was to pull herself out of rationing and thrive, trees had to be felled, drains had to be dug, the hedge had to be erased, and wildlife could go hang.

Natural England, the sense checker of policy and rural social conscience for the Department for Environment, Food and Rural Affairs (Defra), states that between 1946 and 1963 an estimated 4,800 kilometres of English hedgerows were grubbed out per annum. In 1950 the Forestry Commission, taking a rough guess, declared there to be 1 million kilometres of hedgerows in England. By 2007 the Countryside Commission tallied up a mere 477,000 kilometres. The English hedgerow was being eradicated, but not through devilment or the greed of farmers; it was merely a hindrance to production. The emerging, ultimately all-powerful supermarkets demanded more food, for less. The consumer learnt to clamour for the same. Governments of various flavours had become urbanised, as had the voters. The countryside was a foreign country. A vibrant hedge, filled with birdsong, didn't gain votes. Environmentalists, politicians and commentators were all too happy to point a callous-free finger of blame at the farmer for this wrecking of the land, emboldened as they were with their bellies full of plentiful cheap food. The farmers had stark choices: feed the beast and put production before wildlife, or kick back and go to the wall.

Inconsistency is the politician's lot. Since 1945 landowners had been primed and cajoled, encouraged and funded to remove hedgerows. The livestock farmers had duly grubbed out the bullfinch and replaced it with barbed wire. In arable country, the hedges that remained were sad affairs. Filled with gaps, sparse remnants of old. Cut and smashed to sticks in the ground, barely clinging onto life, unloved and of little ecological value. However, in the early 1990s Whitehall called an about-turn. The value of the hedge was once more realised. Not now as a barrier, but as a priceless wildlife habitat. Government grants were made available for planting kilometre upon kilometre of new hedges, frequently in the very places where the previous government's grants had paid to rip them out. The landscape of Suffolk has, over the past twenty-five years or so, become lined with hedging whips guarded with largely ineffective hare- and deer-proof plastic spirals. The new plantings grew, their trunks restricted by their plastic tubes and bare of growth. What should have been hedges became linear rows of leafy lollipops. The upper boughs gave security to some of the birdlife that had so long-missed the hedgerows. Yet these scant-based replacement hedgerows were of no use to the grey partridges or yellowhammer. The small mammals, the voles and dormice, hedgehogs and wood mice, found no shelter here, exposed as they were to predators. The wind and rain could whip through these new havens that were in truth not havens at all, an umbrella frame with no canvas.

To remedy these failings is my lot, to fill the gaps with new growth, to widen and thicken the base and to stiffen the backbone of planted potential. A hedge is only truly a hedge if its foundations are strong. The hedgelayer was once the man who renovated the old. Today I am the man who makes good the new. Ninety per cent of the hedges I lay have been planted within the past twenty years. This is to be celebrated: the hedge has become a thing of veneration once more; a good hedge is as much a mark of a good farmer as is their yield per hectare.

Hedge coppicing is more dramatic than laying. While the

young hedges suit laying well, the older, overgrown hedgerows of earlier times rejuvenate more successfully when coppiced. In this most traditional of East Anglian hedgerow management techniques, I cut the hedge down to a few inches from the ground. All winter the stool that is left will remain dormant, guarded by the cut brash, retained in place by living stakes. Then in the spring nature takes over: fresh growth erupts from the stools, multiple stems rise to the sun. The old and decayed hedge is rejuvenated. It has become a fad with the unenlightened to post images of coppiced hedges on social media, declaring the landowner to be a villain who has 'destroyed' a hedge. This is as far from the truth as is possible. Coppicing is as much working with nature as hedgelaying; we cut down the old so that the new may grow back stronger. It is ironic that those who loudly clamour for 'more wild' are so readily attracted to the order of the laid hedge, yet become red-faced at their keyboards, tweeting and Facebooking their disgust, at the sight and notion of coppice. Hedgelaying is seen as a craft, a timeless artisan activity, one that conjures images of the Green Man. It is these things, but it is neither more nor less regenerative than coppicing; it is simply prettier.

Hedgelaying in all its quirkiness has helped me to gain a level of local notability. Whenever I am introduced to fellow guests at a party as a 'local hedgelayer', they show heartening interest in my work. 'I'd love to learn to do that,' they often reply. 'What a lovely way to earn a living,' they say. Yet this is not a comfortable job – my arms are scratched and scarred, my skin wrecked and snagged by briar, thorn and bramble so often that psoriasis has taken hold. Sometimes I see genuine concern in people's faces. They fear, when they see the angry red scars on my arms, that I am a self-harmer. 'It's not that,' I rush to tell them. 'It's just that life in the hedge is one of constant cuts.' But it is also a joyous one. Few other jobs in the countryside allow you to take a pause from your toil, stand quietly and simply watch the world about you. Hedging brings you so close to wildlife, you cease to merely be an observer; you become as much a part of a hedgerow as a yellowhammer or dormouse. The naturalist observes nature; as a hedger, you are nature. I believe much of my lore and intimate knowledge of hedgerows is not gained through repetitive work – cutting and chopping and bending and pleaching – but in my breaks for breath and pauses for tea. It is only during these quiet times, reflective times, when I truly understand what makes an English hedgerow. My working day is observed closely by mice and voles. Stoats grow used to my activity and dare themselves to come close, to peer myopically at my toil. The birds seem to be nearly impervious to the work; it is no rarity to feel the almost imperceptible weight of a robin land on my bent shoulder; blue tits row up as if in a gallery to gawp at my toil. Grey partridges regard me warily. I sometimes like to think, if only half seriously, that all the creatures know I am doing this for them.

The Perfect Hedge

'What is the perfect hedge?' I'm frequently asked. I hate this question, because my answer is ambiguous at best. 'It is complicated,' I am forced to reply with a politician's swerve. Individual bird, mammal and invertebrate species have so many peculiar hedgerow needs. Height and density matter to birds; yellowhammers want a hedgerow that is thick and low, turtle doves prefer one tall and straggly; every one of the farmland species has its own idiosyncratic requirements. The individual plant species that are present, or not, can be the difference between life and death for some insects. For example, the Brown Elm Tortrix moth, as its name indicates, is brown and likes elm in a hedge. It flies in June and July at dusk and night, wherever elms occur on lowland sites. Its larvae feed nearly exclusively within unopened elm buds, leaving in their wake a characteristic line of holes along a leaf vein, as if an accurate machine gunner had taken potshots. The act of keeping an elm-filled hedge trimmed to a height so that it evades the Dutch elm beetle may enrage people who hate the aftermath of a flail cutter, yet if the hedge were left unmolested and the elms succumbed to the beetle, it would be disastrous for the dowdy Brown Elm Tortrix: the flail for them matters a great deal. The hazel dormouse, like the elm moth, has a name that screams its favoured hedgerow plant. The easiest way to discover a dormouse is to look for hazelnut husks in a field margin bearing a distinctive smooth circular hole. Not only do dormice need hazel; they have somewhat specific requirements for its management. The hazelnuts that they feed on are largely found on more mature uncut plants, yet they prefer to nest in the fresh young regrowth found in recently coppiced hedges. On the multi-award-winning Lodge Farm at Westhorpe in Mid Suffolk, I coppiced some 400 metres of mixed thirteen-year-old hedge for the cousins Patrick and Brian Barker, who farm there. An additional one hundred metres was left untouched, meaning that this somewhat open arable field was not entirely denuded of hedgerow habitat while the cut hedge grew back. We experimented with a variety of dead-hedging methods (which involves replacing the cut hedge brash over the now coppiced stools) to protect regrowth from the attentions of the plentiful hare and deer thereabouts. Two years after coppicing, Patrick Barker and Eliza Leat, a researcher at the RSPB, carried out a bird-nest survey in late autumn along the regrowing line. They discovered two dormice nests nestled within the coppiced hazel stools; holey hazel nutshells, meanwhile, were found near the unmolested length. These nests were the first ever recorded on the farm. A perfect example of the need for mosaics in hedgerow management, and that one size sometimes doesn't even fit one, let alone all.

The greater the variety of plant species in a hedgerow the better, would be a simplistic answer to what constitutes the best hedge. Yet this is not necessarily the case. For example, common elder in a hedgerow, while providing pollen and nectar when it flowers, and plentiful fruit in autumn, is allelopathic, meaning it suppresses other plants growing next to it, a trait that produces gappy hedges, and gappy hedges are poor hedgerows. Equally the spindle is a superb hedgerow plant, producing both flower and fruit; it lays well and responds with vigour after coppicing. The spindle is also the favoured egg-laying plant for a beetle known to science as *Bruchus rufimanus*, known to farmers as the broad-bean bruchid. I learned this from a Suffolk farmer called Ali Driver. He watched me plant 150 metres of native mixed hedging on a farm neighbouring his. After I had finished heeling in the final whip, Ali wandered up, peered into the plastic spiral and said, 'There go the beans!' The hedge has to work with the farm if it is going to be a hedgerow at all.

It is said by some that plant diversity reveals a hedgerow's antiquity. This is known as the Hooper Formula, which advances a hypothesis where the number of woody species in a thirty-yard length of hedge equals the age of the hedge in centuries. The thinking behind Hooper's notion is that the longer a hedge is in situ, the more seeds will have been deposited in it via bird guano, human activity or wind-blow, thereby increasing the varieties present. This does admittedly rely upon the hedge being continuously human-managed, thereby preventing a single species from dominating, as would be the case with field maple in Mid Suffolk, hawthorn in the East Midlands or blackthorn in the West Country. The formula sounds delightful, yet, like a lot of hedgerow-related science, it fails to stand up to close practical scrutiny. In 2019 I was asked to lay a hedge for a Discovery Channel television series called *Born Mucky*. The farmer I was working for was 'Farmer Tom' Martin, a well-known advocate for regenerative agriculture and something of an influencer on agri-social media. The hedge on his farm near Peterborough that I decided to lay for the cameras appeared at first glance to be rather a monster. Dog rose had won the race for dominance, causing the other plants present to dwindle and begin to fail. By the time I had finished clearing out all the bramble and briar by hand, as the director insisted, not only was I puce-faced and covered in cuts but I also discovered I had very little hedge left to lay. In more normal circumstances I would have coppiced such a poor thing as this. I could see it was clearly of some considerable age, judging by the thickness of the hawthorn stumps, and the spindle present had clearly been laid in the past, having tried to become a tree, so gnarled it was at the base. Tom's father, one of the most gentle of men and an ardent local historian, told me later that the hedge followed the track of an ancient pilgrimage route. His records showed that a hedge had certainly been there since the thirteenth century – a small shrine still exists buried within its midst. Seven hundred years of growth, usage and ongoing management with this hedge had resulted in a few scratty ancient thorns and a shoddy spindle or two along with a lot of precocious dog rose and bramble. I'm sure that the Hooper Formula may work in some very specific circumstances, yet despite all of my years spent being in and around hedgerows I have yet to encounter the theory working in practice.

The perfect hedge doesn't exist for the simple reason that Britain and its flora and fauna are so wonderfully and eccentrically diverse. If the perfect hedge exists, it is one that works simultaneously for wildlife and for the farmer. It is my job to ensure that this happy relationship continues to happen.

1

Terroir, the country I know

It is an otherworldly sensation, entering a hedge, as opposed to going around, over or along one. The last three are very human acts that any walker, horse rider or cyclist can do. Yet to physically climb inside a hedge, to be enveloped by the meeting arches of interwoven lattice, the plucking thorns, desiccated leaves, tight-balled nests and bramble, allows you to become a mouse and to join the ranks of hedgepig or weasel. Grown-ups have forgotten this sensation. Adults are stiff and creaky, they find such adventures too sharp and bloody, they fear the spiders, and for their eyes. But for small boys, with scant regard for claustrophobia and dog-rose lacerations, the heart of a hedge is a wonderful world.

I creep in a frog-like crouch, back parallel with the earth and leaf litter. I keep my head lowered, eyes up, to see where I am going, through a flopping fringe. I can see a sliver of cerulean plastic fertiliser sack skewered to a blackthorn spine. For six feet I scrabble and scratch along in my amphibious gait until I reach the marker, pockmarked by a yellow silky ball. Spiderlings erupt into scattering thousands when I touch the flag I had set there as a visual reminder. Beneath the flap of polythene, on the crackling earth, lies a rectangular box. It is partially camouflaged with twigs and leaves; branches of blackthorn provide further top cover. One third of the oblong is a deep, matt, Scots-pine green, the rest an opaque brown. I gingerly creep my arm forward; despite the caution, I still feel the blackthorn's cat claws tug at my skin and raise scarlet weals. My fingers close around the box and I draw it out with even greater care. With no room to move in this prickly tunnel, I leave the way I went in, backwards frogging. My backside and soles reappear out of the hedge, the rest of my skinny body, then a tousled mullet, follows. I kneel briefly on the lushness of the grassy margin, then stand up gratefully. A twig or two falls from my shoulder. I can feel another is caught in my collar and I shake my head like a minkhound fresh out of water. Only now can I hold the trap to the light and see what I have caught. The morning sun filters through the smoky Perspex, silhouetting a mammalian outline. I turn the trap to vertical and with a squeeze of finger and thumb I release two catches. The main body of the trap, with its treadle plate and trap door, comes away in my left hand. In the cup of my palm, the green cubicle contains a bank vole. It squats amidst a few floury husks of porridge oats, the bait I had placed in the device the evening before. The vole quivers silently, staring at me with bulging eyes, black and shining like tailors' pins. The whiskers seem ridiculously long for the snubness of its nose; the shivering goes all the way to the tips. I shuffle the box to evict the little creature into my right hand. A sandpaper-scrape of minute claws on plastic soundtracks the vole's slide into my cupped paw; there is no need to clutch the little mite. There, as I study, it continues to sit, stupefied by the complete horror of this giant creature with giant hands, a giant head and a silly haircut staring down at it. I kneel once more and place the back of my hand at the very edge of the hedge. I fully open my palm, flat like a plate, and the spell is broken. The vole, with an almost imperceptible kick, leaps into the embracing welcome of the emerging leaves and thorns and barbs and spines. I pull out a notebook from the cavernous map pocket of my military-surplus trousers and with a knife-sharpened pencil begin to scribble. I write 15/04/86 in the first column. In the second 'BV/Male'. In the third I mark down 'Hedge 4'. I snap the red-backed book shut, slide it into my trousers and scramble back into the hedge to reset the trap beneath the Fisons sack marker. I then make my way to the next little prison that I have buried deep in this hedgerow atop a bank.

A wren shouts his song at full volume, large lungs in a diminutive feathery egg-shaped frame, clinging with tiny talons to a maple top. A cock blackbird hops in the margin, taking the opportunity to inspect the aftermath of my hedgerow intrusion. Head cocked at ten past two, he grabs some tasty invertebrate morsel – his breakfast is served. My mind strays back to my air gun secreted one hundred yards away in some tussocks at first light. If I crack on there may be time to bag a rabbit before my mother gets cross, for like the blackbird, breakfast is a vital meal in my parents' household and lateness for mealtimes is a strictly punishable crime.

THE HEDGE IS PAROCHIAL, unique to the *terroir* of the condensed and quirky land on which it grows. There is no literal translation of the French word *terroir*. *Terroir* means much more than soil, air or landscape. *Terroir* is the taint of a place, the essence it imbues on man, animal, plant and tree. It mildly annoys me that we have no English for this: is this a national failing? The sheer eccentricity of our national hedgerow network epitomises the variance of *terroir* in the English countryside.

The marketing team at Visit England seemingly feels no shame in lumping 'the countryside' into one self-same blob. Occasionally they'll divide it into upland and lowland, but in general, rural England appears imagined and portrayed as one-size-fits-all. The countryside, thanks to the congruence it receives in print and on screen, has grown increasingly in the minds of the general public as nothing more than the greener, muddier and allegedly more racist place at the edge of the town; the bit that smells a bit odd. In *Politics On the Edge*, Rory Stewart recalls his tenure as environment minister, highlighting that this view filters down from the very top. He recalls Liz Truss saying, 'I don't believe in rural affairs. There is no relevant difference between urban and rural populations.' At the time of speaking, Ms Truss was secretary of state for Defra. The hedgerow evidences the brief-lived former prime minister's error.

Hedgerows refuse to conform to a convenient national stereotype, however troublesome this may be. There are over thirty recognised regional hedgelaying styles to underline this awkward truth. Some hedges are precocious and overly vigorous, others are parched; some are beaten and tardy, or bent and bowed, by the vagaries of wind and wet. Many exhibit extreme variation in their botanic makeup, others boast a single species, the plant capable of winning the race for life there. The hedge compounds its own contrariness in that whilst, like a tree, it mirrors the dual dictators of regional climate and soil, it also reflects, both historically and contemporarily, the idiosyncrasies of a very localised rural industry. Farming, be it arable, vegetable, livestock or mixed, is the deciding factor in how a hedge looks, acts or even whether one is present at all, and the type of farming in turn reflects the regional climate and soil. The Wessex hedges I lived alongside, and within, as a child were enormous affairs, double-rowed blackthorn in the main and frequently set atop a bank. Little wonder that a hedge in the Blackmore Vale, where I went to school, is a monster. Here the soil is a combination of lowland clay in the vales and greensand on the high ground. The vale grows grass with aplomb, being well irrigated by regular rainfall coming in off the English Channel to the south and the Atlantic to the west. The water table is topped up to brimming. Look over this part of Wessex and one word springs to mind – lush. Dorset was, and I think continues to be, overwhelmingly cattle country. A hedge there must be robust, sharp and forbidding, capable of incarcerating a herd of rumbustious bovines each weighing up to 800 kg. A mixed hedge in arable Suffolk can never grow like a Dorset hedge, nor has any need to be like those cavernous bands of Wessex blackthorn.

It is, I suppose, possible to be an expert on hedges, but only in a theoretical context. To claim comprehensive practical authority on the English hedgerow is inconceivable. Hedges are diverse and parochial in their makeup and in their needs and management requirements. The English national network of hedgerows is simply too varied and multifaceted for any one person to assert a hands-on specialism in them all. Similarly, to produce an authoritative book about the English hedgerow would be to write something largely constructed on foundations of theory or reportage, lacking true practical experience. This book focuses on East Anglia – the counties of Suffolk, Norfolk and Cambridgeshire – because this is where I was born and now work, within its hedgerow network. Each season my business partner and I lay, on average, a shade under five kilometres of East Anglian hedgerows. Add to that the 300–400 kilometres of hedgerows we analyse and assess annually for our hedgerow management plans, and I like to think I know the hedges of the east as well as anybody can. Yet I still shy away slightly from the word 'expert'. When it comes to the hedge and when it comes to nature, we are all always learning. We never know it all.

While county boundaries exist, and people are understandably proud of this notional sense of place, they are only mapped as such for administrative convenience. The boundaries that truly matter for the hedge were formed by events occurring long before cartographers, administrators or even humans began farming. Glaciers melting, ancient rivers receding, seas rising and falling and tidal estuaries drying up or flooding over millennia all combined to form the landmass we know as England. These myriad geological and climate changes are acutely distilled in our tiny island, leading to the extremely localised vagaries of soil that we enjoy, or endure. Latterly, the activities of man – our advances and technical improvements in agriculture – have combined with the geographical phenomena to blend and turn each of these folds, valleys, plains and catchments into unique and unrepeatable places, sometimes obviously, frequently subtly idiosyncratic. The variations in our soil, our land use and our hedges lead to an almost impossible challenge of creating a comprehensive yet workable government policy for agriculture and the environmental management of farmland. This is compounded by the backgrounds of the people who debate then create such diktats. The corridors of power are filled with men and women who bring their skills and expertise as lawyers, doctors, bankers, marketeers, management consultants, soldiers or union leaders into play in their new career as members of parliament. Their pre-Westminster knowledge is invaluable. A former GP has coal-face experience when she debates NHS budgets. A former City banker calls out with a confident voice when he sees that the emperor in Number 11 Downing Street is naked. Yet only twelve of the 533 English MPs, at the time of writing, come from a farming background, and none at all, it must be said, were previously professional hedgelayers. It greatly concerns me that fewer than 5 per cent of our politicians, regardless of party, have any direct practical experience of looking after the soil under our feet. It concerns me because, thanks to this dearth of practicality, our hedgerows suffer.

The extreme vagaries of England's soil, and the impact this has on land use, are exemplified within Suffolk's hedgerows. On the western border of this most easterly county lies Newmarket, the headquarters of British horse racing. Here the chalk runs close to the surface and the beech and hornbeam like it that way. In neat, clipped rows of perfection, these three-metre-tall hedges line the expanse of the 'Heath'. This ancient springy turf has, since the reign of James I, been recognised as the best surface bar none for training thoroughbred racehorses. The hedges here meanwhile are a more modern affair. *The Rubbing House*, painted by the father of equestrian art, George Stubbs, in 1765, portrays Newmarket Heath as a sweeping moonscape of spongy sod, punctuated by seemingly random lengths of lonely, white-painted post and rail. In the mid- and foreground stands a brick building or two where the grooms would tend their charges after exercise. Stubbs's eye can be trusted as much as any photographer's of today. The view he saw then was nothing but turf and a mere handful of spindle-shanked horses being waggoned by emaciated grooms while the frock-coated cream of society looked on – eighteenth-century horse racing was indeed the sport of kings. The hedgerows that later emerged, and that continue to bisect Newmarket Heath, reflect the democratisation of horse racing and its growth in popularity, which led to an ever-growing influx of horseflesh into the town. Stubbs's lonely Heath became filled with thoroughbreds and nagsmen; today Newmarket will stable around 3,000 horses in training at a time. The hedges planted on the Heath, with their repeated trimming and retrimming, became nearly impenetrable walls, a practical necessity. Beech and hornbeam cling on to their leaves for almost twelve months of the year; this density helps the work riders keep their highly strung, highly expensive half-tons of galloping horseflesh on the straight and narrow. The hedgerows also maintain secrets, shielding from the prying eyes of gamblers the fitness or otherwise of the red-hot favourite for the 2000 Guineas Stakes. Out of the town, you encounter the studs that breed these paragons of equestrian perfection. Hedges here are similarly thick and tall, now acting as windbreaks and blinds to keep the mares, with costly foals at foot, calm and content. The chalk grows selenium-rich grass, and verdant hedges. Yet these equestrian hedgerows are planted so that no species present might poison a nibbling horse, and their regular mechanical trimming reflects their workday function that suits man and nag alike. The dunnocks and linnets and chaffinches don't care either way. They have shelter from the elements, a place to nest and horse shit to sift through. They thrive in the hedges of racing's HQ.

A mere dozen miles from Newmarket and you leave thoroughbreds and chalk behind. At the most northerly tip of Suffolk, flush on the border with Norfolk, the county dallies briefly with the Fens. Flat as a penny, soil as black as a crow and largely devoid of hedges. A bulge in a line drawn on the map and the word 'Suffolk' (in brackets under the Burnt Fen village sign) is the only evidence that the South Folk of East Anglia play any part at all in the business of peat. The bumping fenland turnpike swiftly smooths, welcoming you to Breckland, a land of sand. Here the hedges are stunted, gapped, hunched and crooked backed, like a line of old men in a bus queue. Scots pine trees string the horizon. The ceaseless 'Breckland Blow' picks up what passes for soil and sandblasts bark. When you lay a Breckland hedge your chainsaw and billhook are blunted in short order; count the rings on the trunk of a thorn and they are as tight as the wrinkles on a chain smoker's face, indicative of a snail-paced growth. Breckland is desiccated, farming here a thankless task. Any plant taller than your knee is savaged by the blow or nibbled to the quick by rabbits – rabbits in their millions; indeed, the rabbit made Breckland what it is, or certainly was. While the soil was nearly useless for crops, the wild rabbits became so prolific that they were commercially warrened. Their meat is a valuable source of protein, and carcases were exported in daily thousands to the towns, hung on hooks in specially run trains. The rabbit skins, meanwhile, were turned to felt, becoming the primary industry in towns such as Brandon and Watton. Great earthy banks were excavated to retain the rabbits, holes dug through them in which traps were set. These sandy mounds were topped with laid furze, turning, over time, into permanent hedgerow features. Myxomatosis saw off most of the rabbits by the mid-1990s, but long before then people had lost their taste for the pale, slightly musky meat, or a crafted felt trilby for that matter.

Yet you can't change the legacy of the bunny in the Brecks, nor the soil, and this unique corner of East Anglia remains largely poor. Farmers have developed, as this innovative tribe does, a method of growing crops here, vegetables for the main. The yearly de-stoning, huge inputs of fertiliser and the constant irrigation required to grow carrots and onions on this thin gritty soil are steadily destroying what was already famine country. Conservationists are desperately trying to reintroduce the rabbit in a bid to cling on to what remains of the old heathland. They will fail because the diseases introduced by man to quell the rabbits are pernicious and now ever present. The warren banks have largely gone, and the furze hedgerows that cling on like a straggling battalion in retreat are on the whole poor old remnants: there is nothing so miserable to my eyes as a Breckland hedge. The Brecks is a harsh landscape, like nowhere else in England, a place that only locals can love, and they do so passionately.

At the south-eastern edge of Breckland lies the Euston estate, seat of the dukes of Grafton, descendants of one of Charles II's ennobled illegitimate children. From thereon, the Breckland sands end, morphing into Ashley Series soils – the High Suffolk clay that forms the breadbasket of Britain. I live here, in the heart of wheat and barley country, alongside which grow sugar beet, beans, oilseed rape and linseed in rotation. The growers of Mid Suffolk will tell you this is no 'boy's soil'. Yet, under a practised hand, this combination of very deep, well-drained, coarse, milk-chocolate-coloured loam is remarkably fertile; wheat yields of eight tonnes to the hectare are feasible. There are a few who are members of the 'ten-tonne club'. In the hedges field maples race ahead, keen to beat all other plants to the punch. Plant a hedge in Breckland's Thetford, and it may take a full century to reach maturity; twenty-five miles away in Mid Suffolk, the same combination of thorn, hazel and guelder rose requires less than a decade to become a dense and meaningful haven for wildlife.

Ancient oaks stand within the Mid-Suffolk hedgerows, spaced at regular intervals and marking parish boundaries, ancient deer parks and the old hundreds. Lines of redundant poplars, planted to become matchwood, lean against one another like drunks; the man from Bryant and May encouraged the landowners to plant them four decades ago, and never bothered coming back to harvest his crop – matches became superfluous when we all stopped smoking. Hedgerows sport gaps, like missing molars, where great elm trees once grew. Nearly all are now long dead. A few leadened skeletons remain, acting as memorials to our country's woeful plant-health security and Dutch elm disease. The suckering remnants of the lost trees still grow, then when they are around sixteen feet high the beetle seems to get in, and the dusty-leafed sons of past greatness turn brown, then wither and die. Our management interventions, either with billhook and saw or tractor-mounted flail, keep the height down and the beetle out. The English elm is rarely a tree any more, but it holds on to life in Suffolk, reduced to the ranks of a nondescript hedgerow plant. The elm moths that rely upon it are grateful. Here, in this part of Suffolk, countless rows of plastic-guarded lollipops have sprung up in the past few decades: hawthorn planted at 70 per cent, and take your pick for the rest – nearly anything grows in the clay. The farmers hereabout have replanted much of what their fathers and grandfathers dug up in the post-war rush to grow food.

Proceed eastward and the fecundity continues, until you reach the Suffolk Broads at Bungay and Beccles. Cattle graze the water meadows, finding shelter beneath crenulated crack willows. Marshland, bisected by machine-cut dykes fringed with reed, is home to curlew, snipe and wild pink-footed and white-fronted geese, along with countless duck. Broadland hedges sport holly, dogwood and blackthorn, happy with their feet in the wet. Maple too is present, but growing without the rapacious vigour seen a mere few miles inland on the mid-county clay. South of the Broads lies the Sandlings. This too is heathland, yet quite unlike that seen in the Brecks, being liberally dusted by the salt of the North Sea. Once, this slightly acidic, sandy soil was sheep country; now, like Breckland, it is for the main ploughed, de-stoned and irrigated; veg grows here along with vast fields of herbs and maize. The hedges of the Sandlings are a hotchpotch, frequently bare in the bottom with the soil blown away in winter's easterly gales that scream without hindrance from Siberia. There are belts of Scots pine, bracken and clumps of gorse that sit like a musky yellow crown on the high ground; Dartford warbler, goldfinch and linnet grip on to the savage spikes. In the hedgerows, buckthorn, spindle and guelder rose take a second-string role to the more dominant blackthorn. You'll find hawthorn here, but it seems to sulk, regardless of species: all leaves are coated with a fine dust, as are the roads, houses, tractors and cars. The Sandlings is well named.

Silly Suffolk they call us, and maybe we are. Yet this county, while mapped and flagged as one place, has multiple *terroirs* of incredible diversity and variance. Breckland is a foreign country to High Suffolk. The Sandlings may as well be the moon when compared with the Broads. And the stark variations of soil and the impact this has on our agriculture, land use, and therefore our hedgerows, is a story repeated in all forty-eight English counties. To fully understand the hedgerows of England, to glean their needs and foibles, it is essential their managers are parochial; they must be 'of' the *terroir*, ingrained in the soil and climate, land and people. To become a hedger, you don't need to be a farmer, but you do need to understand farming and farmers. A hedger must love the hedge, and the wildlife that calls farmland home, but it must be a pragmatic love, never idealistic or overly romantic. The hedger's relationship with farmers is tight, these are our clients, our paying punters. Yet the farmer, for the hedger, is much more than a mere source of funding. The farmer is integral to our work. Without agriculture and the farmer there never would have been any hedges at all.

2

Practical Conservationists

I follow Richard Gould closely as we walk up the hedgerow together; the dew is off the grass now, thanks to a warming sun. I watch his eyes, his facial expressions and his body language. He is hunting. Not in a red-coated, horn-blowing way. Richard was a gamekeeper, and his tribe are markedly more calm and considered when searching for prey. His gaze flickers back and forth over the tangle of grasses and bramble that twine and clamber into the crossed wands of hawthorn, hazel and field maple. It is as if he is reading a book at pace. He stops abruptly and I just avoid bumbling into him. He points at a tunnel; the grass is parted. To me, it looks the same as any of the other myriad tunnels that appear like eye sockets in the thatch of tussock in the hedge bottom. 'Doe rat,' he mutters, as much to himself as to me. 'We want rid of that one.' His fingers make a walking motion and I track their path, which traces a barely distinguishable runway across the tussock grass. Now made aware, I too begin to read the story Richard sees. A doe rat has made her way along the root system of the hedge. Guarded from avian dangers by the thick top cover, she has had to break this safe embrace and make her way across an open and therefore potentially deadly space. It is a risk she is prepared to run;

she has kits to feed. Her goal is a cerulean-blue drum, fixed and raised off the ground on splayed wooden legs. This garish splash of primary plastic in a sea of gentler tones is a feeder filled with wheat. A spring-like metal spiral hangs from the underside of the barrel. This permits pheasants and partridges to peck for food and the smaller songbirds to clear up after them, like table-sweeping under-waiters in a restaurant. Next to this larger feeder, a green bucket-like container is screwed to a fence post. Small metal ports provide access and perches for passerines to feast on the supplementary feed inside. The scattered grains also attract the rats. For a maternal rat, the wheat is a mere snack to keep her topped up as she hunts for more nutritious fare. A buck rat is a scabrous disease-spreading spoiler of foodstuffs, a pest in the sense of being a greedy, costly nuisance. The female of this tribe has all of these traits and more. When feeding young or when pregnant – which are the two permanent states a doe inhabits from six weeks old until she dies – she is a hunter. This mother likes to feed her youngsters on fresh meat; a whitethroat's egg is acceptable, a grey partridge egg is perfect. 'We definitely want that one gone,' Richard repeats. I wander onto my truck, which is parked some hundred yards away in the shade of some blackthorn scrub. Opening the tailgate, there is a scent of bovine-like chainsaw oil, sweet petrol and woodchip. I put on surgical gloves – rats know all too well that the scent of man means danger – and then I remove a matt-black wooden box, a plastic bucket and a spade from the tangle of saws and feed bags that litter the back of my disgraceful vehicle. I carry them back to where Richard stands, his hand resting on the feeder, eyes scanning again, hunting once more. Wielding the spade, I carve out some soil from the bank against which the feeder stands. I try the box for size in the crumbling, earthy space. Dissatisfied, I enlarge the hole and try once more, to better effect. Inside the wooden box a DOC trap is bolted to the floor. DOC is an acronym for New Zealand's department of conservation, a country that has little truck with invasive predators and has therefore developed a devastating solution for their control. The trap is a wicked thing. The spring takes significant force to set, and when sprung sweeps down with such stark fury that it leaves a hollow in my stomach at the thought of fingers caught in the blunt jaws. I set the trap, hiding my fear, knowing that Richard is watching my movements with scrutiny. I take a generous handful of peanuts and maize kernels from the plastic bucket and sprinkle them over the trap's trigger plate, then close the hinged lid of the box, securing it with a carabiner. This soulless instrument of death is now primed. I sprinkle soil around the sides of the box and crumble more between my palms at the entrance. I then cover the whole thing with hedge fronds that snap like crackers; it looks like a hole in the bank. It is only now that I look up at Richard again. He is kind enough not to criticise my amateurish attempts. We walk on, he still hunts, and I still watch.

RICHARD GOULD IS A Norfolk boy. Formerly a gamekeeper, he is now my business partner. I have the lion's share of expertise when it comes to laying hedges; he brings his hard-earned knowledge as a naturalist, woodsman and coppicer. Our similarities and differences in skill set and personality combine, ensuring our work makes a positive impact for game and wildlife. Richard used to toil for others, but like a released bird, he seems to now relish the same sense of freedom that I experienced when I left behind the stuffy rigidity of life in the Household Cavalry.

Gamekeepers are a fascinating if roundly maligned breed. The keeper has long been on the receiving end of a lot of hatred. Both Victorian and Edwardian scribes delighted in portraying the gamekeeper as the lord's lackey, a class traitor who set man traps, spring guns, and kept half-wild mastiffs to crunch and maim the plucky poacher. The poacher, on the other hand, they romanticised, crafting him into a working-class hero with a lineage stretching back to Robin Hood – a rogue, yet at heart an honest hungry peasant, artfully netting the gammon-faced squire's hares or bagging his plentiful game to feed his own downtrodden family as was his birthright. This narrative was part of the townsman's growing sneer towards those who had chosen to stay behind in the countryside, when sharper, more urbane adventurers had followed the money to the town. The keeper was the lickspittle, a Guy of Gisborne, the very epitome of a despised middleman-cum-policeman in the rural hierarchy. The narrative was born during a period of mass economic migration from the country – rural incomers swelled the towns and cities. In 1851, 43 per cent of the English population lived in rural parishes, by 1931 it was a mere 19 per cent. The gamekeeper was the embodiment of what these new urbanites hated most, an unwelcome reminder of their own recent hairy-heeled, yokel past, where the social order of villages was entrenched and unbending. A place where caps were doffed to landowners and senior estate staff were addressed with a prefix of 'Mister' upon pain of a thick ear.

Doubtless not all gamekeepers are arch naturalists like Gouldy. In truth, some are more akin to glorified chicken farmers, rather than 'guardians of the land' as the simplistic Countryside Alliance dubs all of them. The demands of commercial shooting require keepers to produce and release game-farm-reared pheasant and red-legged partridge poults. The human resource and sheer number of birds required to create a commercially viable shoot are such that shooting needed to industrialise itself, little different from modern farming. Quite how many millions of game birds are released each year is a touchy subject. Anti-shooters postulate a figure of up to 70 million, the shooting world says it's more like 10 million. The precise figure is in truth unknown. It probably sits somewhere in the middle. Many of these commercial shoots are excellent examples of landscape-scale conservation; some are at best neutral in their biodiversity, a few are a downright disgrace, just as damaging to the environment as any other industry that solely takes and never gives back to the land. The positive ecological benefits that shoots undoubtedly bring, through the cover crops they plant, the habitats they maintain, the supplementary feeding they undertake and the predators that are controlled, are counterbalanced by the stocking of game. If overstocking takes place in a bid to raise revenue this leads to an increase in parasites. Ground flora in woodland becomes denuded. Margins near to release sites become devoid of invertebrate life. And a few gamekeepers are raptor killers. They are criminals, readily prepared to poison and trap species that are protected by law. The fact that these criminals and the overstocked wastelands of greedy shoots are a miniscule exception, rather than the norm, matters nought to those who seek to end shooting. For them the gamekeeper is a tool, a handy stooge to aid their narrative that all is rotten in the countryside. It is a simple tale to tell, told to an audience who most likely have never met a gamekeeper in their lives (good, bad or indifferent) – the keeper carries a gun, bad people carry guns, ergo keepers are bad people. The other tools of the gamekeeper's trade are similarly portrayed as instruments of heartless death, used with malice. The modern traps we use, such as the DOC 150 that Richard Gould watched me place, are as clinical as a surgeon's scalpel. However, the images of trapping, posted on Twitter (X) by animal rights activists, are of bloodied and rusting snaggle-toothed tools of yesteryear. These pictures capture voyeuristic social media likes, leading the viewer to draw a conclusion that these museum pieces are still in daily use. Snares that hold foxes are declared to be garottes; poisons, we are told, are spread with abandon; and any creature, be it furred or feathered, is ruthlessly destroyed. It is a beguiling story, and it fills newspapers year in, year out.

Gouldy once told me a tale from when he was still keepering. He had been rushed to hospital, having smashed one of his legs to shards in an accident involving a tractor trailer. Lying in his ward bed, heavily doped on painkillers, he overheard one of the nurses on the other side of the curtains that were closed around his bed stage-whispering to a colleague, '*That's the one who does the horrible job.*' 'What the fuck?' I blurted. 'I hope you complained?' Gouldy shrugged. His reply was laced with his ready stoicism. 'People don't like keepers, they never have.'

There is a gaping flaw in the 'heartless gamekeeper' script, of course – it is largely a total nonsense. Richard Gould, and keepers of his ilk, are not integral players in our charge to bring nature recovery because they are adept at *killing* animals and birds; rather, their genius lies in keeping them *alive*. Most keepers were the sort of children who kept baby birds in shoeboxes and fed them mealworms. They know which birds nest where, and can read the tussocky margins, the woods and hedgerows, like others do a book. Keepers go into this vocation not through bloodlust but because of an overwhelming fascination with nature. Richard is a naturalist, a very fine naturalist, yet he endlessly worries, believing he is scorned by others in the conservation movement because his CV lacks formal qualifications. He frets because he holds no degree in ecology, biology or any other *ology*. But his own perceived scholastic failings mattered little to the judges of the 2018 Purdey Awards. These awards are the 'Oscars' of game and wildlife conservation. The judges created an extraordinary prize for him, an unprecedented occurrence, in order to recognise Gouldy's almost super-human efforts on behalf of the grey partridge and its conservation. For all this, I still find myself repeatedly having to reassure him that his absence of academic honours is a proficiency, not a failing. His classroom was hedgerow and woodland, not a lecture hall. He learned the ways of wildlife not from dons, but as an apprentice to time-served naturalist keepers. He has never stopped learning; fieldwork for him is his daily ritual, not an hour's break from a desk. This is not to say that scientists are not vital partners in farmland wildlife conservation. They are. It would, however, be fair to say that the technologists receive an unequal level of trust and credence when compared with their more artisanal compatriots. Since the end of the Second World War, government policy on farmland wildlife conservation and land management has hung upon the words and data provided by scientists. The biodiversity decline that is evident to all us laymen has happened on their watch. It was the chemist, after all, who created the pesticides, fungicides and chemical fertilisers, not the spray operator. It was the biologist who unearthed the methodology to eke out the last strands of goodness from the soil, not the farmer. The geographer, not the hedgelayer, was the person who hypothesised that, if the hedgerows were removed, we could increase cropped field areas by a meaningful factor. For policy makers, the Arcadians, with their generations of minute observations and lived experience, were, and continue to be, largely regarded as purveyors of hearsay or heresy, their words dismissed with a waft as 'anecdotal evidence'. The academics' data, meanwhile, is treated as gospel truth.

The obsession with science over experience seems a peculiarly Western phenomenon. Further east, there is a long history of including practitioners in national decision-making on farming; there is no reticence to 'ask the fellows who cut the hay', a line that comes from an ancient Chinese poem *The Decade of Sheng Min*, translated by the poet Ezra Pound. It was used by the folklorist George Ewart Evans as the title for his chronicle of the country people of Blaxhall in Suffolk, whom he interviewed in the mid-1950s. As youths, his subjects ploughed, cultivated and drilled using horses, in middle age with steam engines, and as grizzled veterans with diesel tractors. In one generation of agricultural maelstrom these people had toiled and tilled the land; they learned and they adapted. This cornucopia of accumulated lore and experience Ewart Evans collated and retold faithfully, without embellishment or opinion. As a social history it is fascinating, but for farmland conservationists the book is essential reading, a litany of time-won knowledge of fur, feather, fin and soil. The people Ewart Evans interviewed would have laughed out loud if they heard themselves described as wise men and women: they were, after all, just recounting their life stories. They had little if any book learning. They had no clue what a *Lepus europaeus Pallas* was, yet you would back them to find the brown hare's form with nonchalant ease. Through their daily toil in this Suffolk landscape, they became a part of that landscape. It became ingrained, imbuing them with *terroir*. A good gamekeeper is part of the *terroir*, he knows the land because he is *of* the land; he becomes of the land.

Gouldy and I have a ritual. Each morning, we draw up our trucks alongside a hedge and prepare to start our work. Our Isuzu pickups are identical models, mine a filthy heap, his pressure-washed daily and diligently tidied. A sickly-sweet air freshener moulded in the shape of a jelly bean wafts out its stench, stuck across an air vent. We know we should immediately start our work; after all, time is money for the self-employed hedger, and daylight in winter is in short supply. Yet we don't start work. We first let our dogs out for a sniff and a stretch, then he and I prevaricate and chatter. We sit on our tailgates, sipping from Thermos flasks; mine contains sweet black tea, Richard's an espresso-strength treacly brew of coffee. I put down my cup and spit on my billhook blade, rubbing in a circular motion with a whetstone. I don't bother to watch the gritty, grey lozenge-shaped stone as it sharpens the edge to a razor; this is an automatic action, no different from tying the laces of my boots. The grind and snick of the sharpening stone doesn't interrupt our confab, a mixture of gossip, rumour and specula-tion. It is a précis of the previous night's news, gleaned from the rural jungle drums that sound out on WhatsApp groups and social media platforms – the modern-day village pump. We talk of suspicious vehicles observed on farm security cameras and tut over night-time poachers discovered lamping deer. We enjoy our daily gnash over the latest pronouncements from some faceless government department or NGO quango. However, buried like treasure beneath our groans and moans and whines, there are rare jewels of natural brilliance. I serve up my observations to Gouldy, and he smashes back an artful return. His years of keepering have made him an expert in the ways of the living denizens of hedgerows. He may not be able to reel off, like I have trained myself to do, the names of the LBJs (Little Brown Jobs, the catch-all term for the finches, tits and passerines who seethe and tweet in our hedges) but by God he knows them for all that. Gouldy pricks up his ears like his labrador Oz. A hysterical blackbird shouts *chang, chang, chang*. 'Stoat,' Gouldy says. 'How do you know that?' I scoff. '*Chang, chang, chang* is danger on the ground,' he replies. '*Chit, chit, chit* is danger in the air.' I watch the hedge where the blackbirds fret and where we are about to start work. I peer through binoculars until my eyes water. Sure enough, I spy the lithe fidget auburn slip of a hunting stoat as it appears from beneath an old elm stump. You don't learn this in a classroom, I think to myself, you learn this by osmosis, by being part of the natural order. 'Lucky guess!' I tell Gouldy. He shakes his head. The corners of his mouth raise slightly. He knows I am taking the piss, another daily ritual. We put our dogs away, screw cups back onto flasks and start earning money.

Our rituals continue in the hedge. This one is sited some thirteen miles as the rook flies from Ewart Evans's Blaxhall. Gouldy works the chainsaw. He is as fastidious with the Stihl as he is with his Isuzu. Each evening, before he goes into his kitchen, he disappears into his cavernous workshop. There he rasps the chain with precision, filing it to a honed pitch. He uses an airline to blow out the previous day's sawdust, and cleans the filters. The fuel cans he fills and mixes with a cocktail barman's precision. The bar oil is topped up, free from woody detritus. Now, he begins to wield his screaming orange-and-white 241, and sides up the outer-facing limbs of a thorn. His face is hidden behind a helmet's mask, his ears muffled, and we need no words. I have grown completely used to his ways and his methods. I wait until he flicks the saw's safety bar forward, and only then do I lean in and drag out and bundle up the new-cut brash in a prickly embrace. The armful is thrown behind us onto a wide grass margin, there to join countless other bundles, forming a wall of cut limbs, curling briar and dead wood. In a week or two it will dry, then, heaped by a tractor's front forks, it will be burned, crackling and spitting in a brief inferno.

Once Gouldy has cleared out, we set about laying the hedge. It is 175 metres in length, a woodland-ride edge. Laying will thicken things up, creating a windbreak and letting light into the ride. Quelling the breeze suits the creatures who call this wood home – no one and nothing likes a chill on its back, and light means woodland wildflowers will erupt. Gouldy makes a right-to-left downwards diagonal cut with the Stihl. He stops a few inches from the ground. I reach over his roached back to grab the pleacher with a gauntleted hand; it bends willingly. With my steady tug the limb folds, a gentle creak sounds through my ear protection, and I lay the pleacher at a forty-degree angle. I have already half driven a hazel stake into the September soil, crisp-baked from summer's drought. Stretching to my left is a row of fellow stakes, not guardsman straight in their rank: no line is perfectly plumb in nature, even with a man-made hedge. The pleacher is placed in front of the nearest stake, then I swing my billhook and chop a nick, which allows me to bend the shorn thorn behind the next stake. I tidy the nick, leaving a clean ivory scar that will in time heal over; the bark will callous, and all will be well. I roll my wrist and snick off a few side- and down-facing shoots with the blade. I then pick up my sledgehammer, a seven-pound lump, and whack the stake home, tightening up the now-tamed hedge. While I do this the chainsaw roars again next to my right ear. Gouldy nips off the heel of the laid pleacher, angling his bar. This ensures rainwater will run off rather than pool on the cut stump. Fail to do this and the man-handled living thorn will become a dead twig by the time warming spring recalls the sap. We make a stride to the right and repeat the process with the next limb, then the next and the next and the next. Any mechanical difference in our actions is dictated by a change in plant species. Hazels crowd together in stools and require judicious coppicing to find the right limbs to lay. Spindle tears and breaks with impunity. Old hawthorn tends to be dead in the middle, with only the cambium living, and therefore is laid with tender care. Maple is boys' work; it is forgiving and easy, that is until the hard frosts come, when it becomes as brittle as greenhouse glass. Blackthorn is kindly – a child could lay blackthorn – but its suckers are many and the verdigris barbs stab through the thickest of gloves. We work in this methodical way, the saw's racing chain tearing away mere feet from my hands or head. Gouldy is the only man I would trust to this degree. If he messes up, I die. Chainsaws can kill and it's not all that rare that they do – an average of eight people are killed in chainsaw-related accidents annually in the UK. Likewise, if I miss a cut with my billhook, he will sustain a hideous wound. If he's unlucky I may hit a vein; he'd bleed out in this thorny brash-filled ditch before I'd even dialled three nines on my phone. Ours is a dangerous occupation, made safe, as much as such work can ever be safe, thanks to our relationship of trust and mutual reliance on each other – that and our time-earned competence with these tools.

Lunch sees us back on the tailgate, legs waggling like children on a village-green swing. We talk and we talk at lunch. I am a talker at the best of times, and the lengthy periods of chainsaw-induced silence leave my thoughts pent up and blocked like a damned stream. Richard is similar. He explodes, blurting out his thoughts, interrupting my flow, talking at a sometimes-unfathomable tangent to the topic I had been expounding on. If there is one thing I could strangle him quite happily for, it is his interruptions. I am so certain that my views must be heard first and foremost. Yet for all that, his thoughts are always worth hearing. For a man so reticent about displaying his intellect, he is more than a mere font of wisdom on rural life and natural lore; he is well read and a deep thinker. I remember us once sitting alongside a fenland hedge, sipping tea, watching a hunting marsh harrier and listening in silence to his remedy for our national nature decline. I thought to myself as I picked up my tools to restart after Gouldy had finished his lecture, more's the pity that environment ministers aren't treated to a tailgate conversation with him. We wouldn't be half so buggered as we are now.

We use an inordinate quantity of stakes and binders when laying a hedge. A hedge 175 metres in length requires us to coppice, point up and transport out of the wood some 220 of the two-inch-thick, six-foot-tall straight rods. As a rule of thumb, a hazel stake is hammered home every eighty centimetres in a laid hedge, which is measured, more or less, by the distance between my elbow and the tip of my middle finger. Hazel is superior to ash and sweet chestnut, but on a par with sycamore, this now honorary native tree species being extremely commonplace in East Anglian coppice woods. Binders are three metre- or more whippy lengths. These are woven in bundles of two (three if it's a posh hedge) between the stakes, making the laid hedge a more stable beast. Coppicing is a poor-paying necessity for hedgelayers. It is curious that the benefits brought to woods and wildlife by hazel coppicing go financially unrewarded either by Defra or most of the landowners we work for. Such was the case with our sourcing the raw materials for this job. The farmer was doing us a favour by giving us a coup of his well-managed wood from which to glean our stakes and binders. The quality of the material was such that it was easier work than usual: 90 per cent of each hazel clump produced spars sufficiently straight to make a neat job and perfectly pliable binders.

We had coppiced in this wood before, harvesting some 500 binders and a similar number of stakes the previous winter. It is what is termed an SSSI by Natural England. These 'sites of special scientific interest' are deemed so because they are species-rich places, managed so that nature comes first, not always a favourable state of affairs for farming or, bizarrely, for the woods themselves. Woods such as this are rare in Suffolk. Ours was never a particularly wooded county, and over the millennia much of the old woods and forestry were felled to make way for sheep or the plough: farming is always dependent upon what the financial markets require. In our ritualistic way, Gouldy and I had stopped for elevenses. No vehicles are allowed in this wood in winter – the tearing tyres would damage the delicate flora found in the rides. Gouldy parked his backside on an upturned bucket, I rested on a stump.

Within a matter of minutes, the birds in the wood recommenced their chatter, having been silenced in the roar of chainsaws as we coppiced our bounty. In December, birdsong is not the raucous, showy affair of spring. It is less competitive. Blue and great tits have conversations, goldcrests gossip, even the habitually hysterical blackbirds calm down, uttering half-hearted *chits* or *changs* according to what has disturbed them. Green woodpeckers, meanwhile, scream a year-round manic *yaffle*. A wheeling buzzard over our heads was similarly consistent – his mewing as grating as someone else's grizzling child. The herring gulls that circled alongside the raptor kept quiet; on the wing they are content to watch rather than comment. A covey of grey partridges out on the plough *kerred* contentedly – this farm is rare in the high numbers it holds. Linnets and yellowhammers, wrens and dunnocks cheeped, chirped and hissed in the woodland edge. Then, all of this subdued avian background prattle ceased in a start. The stark change made us look up from our reflections in steaming cups. On the far side of the wood from us, two human shapes appeared. Noisy humans, rustling and crackling the brash as they walked with a sloping tread, past stools of hazel, towering oaks and clumps of bramble and self-set thorn. These interlopers were loud in every way. The hi-viz outfits they wore, so jarring and out of place, fitting for road menders, perhaps, but not for woodland walkers. They marched, talking to one another, neither appearing to look at the wonders about them. We could see one carried a tablet computer, both had binoculars slung low around their necks, each step causing them to swing like dual pendulums. 'Morning,' I said. Gouldy nodded his welcome. Oz growled – something I had never heard the genial old canine gentleman do before. He tucked his tail under his bum. 'What are you up to? Out for a walk?' I quizzed the couple, who seemed intent on marching by without stopping. 'Bird habitat survey,' the lady replied.

This lit a glimmer of memory. A water company had bought the liquid rights to our region at the time of country-wide privatisation, and now it was planning to construct a multi-billion-pound pipeline to bring high-pressure water from damp Lincolnshire into dehydrated Norfolk and Suffolk. The dazzling orange male of the pair began to explain, as if reading from a crib sheet, that they were surveying a 350-metre-wide buffer zone along the entirety of the proposed route. 'One of the largest projects of its kind,' he concluded, in a tone that suggested he was expecting us to break into applause. I asked the question I imagine most ecologists are asked when they meet land-workers: 'Have you seen anything interesting?' 'No, nothing of note,' said the hi-viz lady. Her face looked chilled, strands of dark hair falling from beneath her ill-fitting helmet. 'Not surprising really. This really isn't a very good habitat,' the man interjected, speaking over his colleague. I could feel Richard bristle; 'Really,' he said, without any hint of a question. Gouldy and I watched the pair slope off, resuming their walking and talking. Richard has old-fashioned manners. He waited until they were out of hearing distance. Then he let fly a stream of profanities, incensed and incredulous at the lack of fieldcraft, at the seeming absence of basic bird- and habitat-recognition skills, at the overall oddness of it all.

Later that day, as we manhandled and bundled our binders and stakes out of the wood, the ecologists came to mind once more. Had they, we wondered, really missed the red-listed species that flew before their clumsy tread? Had they failed to see the coasting herring gulls? Did they mistake the woodcock that jinked across the ride for a woodpigeon? Surely they saw the covey of grey partridges that were jugged on the plough nearby? Did they miss those dunnocks and linnets? Were they unaware that this is an SSSI wood, a rare jewel of well-managed hazel coppice and veteran oaks? Possibly. Or was there another reason why they did not see any birds or nesting habitat? For every one of the countless housebuilding or infrastructure projects that proliferate in England, it is enshrined in law that an ecological survey must take place before work may commence; these surveys must be undertaken by individuals 'suitably qualified for the task'. If rare species are recorded or delicate habitats found by these suitably qualified ecologists, mitigation must be made by the construction companies. We are informed by the Green Party, the RSPB, the Wildlife Trusts, environmental journalists and commentators that the UK is the most nature-depleted country in Europe. I struggle to find substantiated independent evidence to support their statements. That is not to say I believe all is rosy and wildlife is thriving. I work in the landscapes these ecologists survey. I see first hand that many species of flora and fauna have experienced significant declines in the past four decades. For some, such as the grey partridge, lapwing, dunnock and starling, that decline has been near-catastrophic. Only the blind or the wilfully ignorant would believe otherwise.

However, the statistics and data that are cited to underline Britain's status as the 'most nature-depleted country in Europe' are all provided by ecologists such as those who disturbed our tea break. The data they collect is passed up to desk-bound colleagues, who check it, edit it and pretty it up. The resulting presentation, with its columns of ticks in boxes, method statements and high-resolution photography, is made palatable and ready for consumption by local government bodies. Following a meeting or two, the survey moves on up the food chain to national government administrators. There the data and the findings are analysed and, in theory, if nature is indeed found to be threatened by the digging of water pipelines, the erection of power cables, or 300 almost identical mock-Georgian four-bedroomed executive homes, then checks, balances, mitigations and vetoes are supposedly put in place.

The ecologist who notes a supposed absence of habitat or wildlife is, therefore, a very useful and indeed profitable individual for some. For small-scale property developers through to multinational utilities giants, healthy habitats and rare wildlife are not wondrous at all; instead they are profit-sapping challenges that need to be overcome. The discovery of willow tit nesting habitat in coppice woods, hedgerows that are perfect for yellowhammers or wet corners stuffed with great crested newts are delightful for the naturalist. Yet for the builders of roads, water pipelines, electricity pylons, solar farms and housing estates, and their shareholders, this rare flora and fauna spells ruin for the bottom line. Far better for them that the narrative of 'nature-depleted', 'sheep-wrecked' or 'chemical-soaked arable wasteland' continues and is advanced as a norm for the British countryside. How delighted a minister for housing, energy or transport is when he or she can report to the House that more homes will be built, train speeds will increase and water will flow more efficiently, and all that accomplished with a clean conscience because the ecology report concluded that the land consumed by these infrastructure projects contains 'nothing of note'.

I only begin to bind the hedge when the last pleacher is laid. Gouldy refuses to get involved in this final part of the proceedings. He claims he can't do it. I know that is not true. I am in two minds whether his reluctance is down to binding being a fiddly, somewhat arty skill, or whether he indulges me because he knows I rather enjoy the fiddling and the artiness. Either way he is happy to leave me alone while I weave and bend binders. He follows behind, cutting each stake at a regulation angle and identical height to its neighbour. All that is left is to tidy the last of the brash and chop any firewood we have gleaned, throwing the logs into the back of our trucks – we work in happy communion. I snap some photographs to provide visual evidence for the bean counters at the Rural Payments Agency (RPA), a final pre-requisite of working under Defra grants. 'Where are we tomorrow?' I ask Gouldy. 'Wyken,' he replies, adding, 'that long length from Burnt Firs.' I can't remember for the life of me where Burnt Firs is. For me, so much of this landscape in which we work, with its archaic names for fields and coverts and lanes, melds into one in my middle-aged mind. However long I live here, I feel I will never completely be of this *terroir*. But Gouldy is. Very much so.

3

Plan then Plant

I raise a third finger behind my back and continue to pace and count the margin in measured metre strides. My chin sits on my right collarbone as I walk, in a militaristic 'eyes right'. As I walk, I scrutinise the hedge and mutter into my top pocket where my phone is tucked – the dictation app, with pricked electronic ears, listens to every word. 'Hawthorn, maple, blackthorn, dog rose, hazel, gap of twenty metres,' I mutter. This wonder of technology is a new discovery. It transcribes my spoken words into text; no longer do I need to fumble along trying to quadruple-task, counting, photographing, assessing and writing down my findings in a notebook as I walk and measure and prescribe interventions, the core activities in gathering data for hedgerow management plans. I stare at the stark gaps, briefly halting next to a maple that has monstrously raced ahead of its neighbours, more tree than hedge now. 'That'd lay,' I mutter to myself and to my dog, who scuffles about a well-trained five metres from my heel. I criticise and note and make plans in my mind, seeing these holes made whole once more. I envision pleachers laid and stakes driven in, the tops bound and bare lengths gapped up with new whips, guarded in plastic spirals and held in place by bamboo canes. My little finger, broken and arthritic, more crippled than the others, crookedly rises from my fist. 'Four hundred metres,' I mouth into the phone. Twenty-five more strides and I reach the right angle of the field end. I peer over the boundary to my front. A shimmering flock of pigeons feeds out on the stubble through which the first green shoots of oilseed rape show in dusty green. I am more than 200 metres away but the birds who stand on guard, on the periphery, pop up their heads and stare, braced for exit, always wary. They decide that eating, not flight, is the best course of action and they get back to it. Woodpigeons are cautious gluttons. I look up to watch more scud in. With the wind at my back, and up their arse, the speeds they achieve never cease to amaze. I read somewhere that a bloke in Berkshire, a pigeon shooter most likely, had clocked one travelling at over 90 mph – little wonder I miss so many when I try to shoot them in February in the woods. A steady trickle of these masters of speed, greed and resilience pass overhead to join the feeding frenzy. Each circles the nodding throng on the ground in turn before flaring into the wind with a matador flourish. Pigeons maintain their social distance from those already feeding. I'll tell Gouldy when we meet back at our trucks for a tailgate lunch – we may go pigeon shooting tomorrow. I look down at my phone once more, mind back on the job of hedgerow management plans. I open the dictation app to check what the gadget thinks I said. 'Awesome, maypole, blackthorn, dog onse, hay sell, cap cough twenty,' it reads, then, 'that wood day.' Technology is a wonderful thing. I pull out my notebook and begin to write my findings from memory. I have many more miles to walk yet. The sun is getting high and Mabel is panting five metres ahead.

GOULDY AND I DRAW a close on hedgelaying in mid to late March. Because it is around now that the squabbling and the mayhem of nesting season begins. Robins, dunnocks and blackbirds are the most precocious of birds when it comes to parenthood. Invariably it is the discovery of one or other of their tightly woven nests, containing three or four aquamarine eggs, that leads us to lay up our saws and oil our billhooks for another season. Robins and blackbirds are common (the dunnock now tragically not), yet destroying any of this parental beak-work is hardly the action of a conservationist. A Defra diktat anyway demands that we must finish hedgelaying by 1 April and we leave the hedges of the farms and the estates untouched until next September, when the process rolls on once more in the never-ending cycle that makes up our lives. This doesn't mean that our management ceases. The clocks change, the days lengthen, and it's time to start planning.

Jeremy Squirrel is like many of our farming clients – he only discovered he was a conservationist when we told him he was one; before that he dismissed his efforts as 'just being a farmer'. It must be said at this point that any farmer called Jeremy Squirrel who isn't conservation-minded would be a travesty, proving there is no poetry left in this world. Jeremy farms on the way to the wool towns: these are the crazily angular and ancient conurbations such as Clare, Long Melford, Cavendish and Lavenham. Here Suffolk shuns its reputation for being flat and the land rolls and dips, flirting with Essex over on the wrong side of the Stour. The wool towns boast monolithic churches, which reveal a fascinating turn of England's agricultural history. It was witch-hunting country and the overtly outsized buildings boast of the region's fifteenth-century wealth, and the importance and piety of a handful of wealthy local patrons. These ecclesiastic displays of affluence were all affordable thanks to the humble sheep. Suffolk boomed between 1450 and 1530 on the back of the wool trade. Local lords argued for and achieved tariff-free trading for Suffolk cloth merchants. Ninety per cent of the entire county's workforce became employed in some shape or form by wool, from shepherding to weaving, from spinning to dying. Such was Suffolk's wool strength that the county was not only able to nearly single-handedly supply the nation's cloth requirements, but also traded widely in Europe and Russia. Merchants' houses proliferated in villages that transformed into towns; lofty guildhalls were erected to proclaim the power and influence of wool. Meantime, out in the fields, land that had been strip-farmed from the Anglo-Saxon period through to the mid-Middle Ages on a part serf, part self-employed contractor basis, was taken back in hand by the landlords. The individualism of small-tenanted plots morphed to mirror a system we would more or less recognise today, with wealthy individuals or organisations (usually universities or the church) owning the land and employing others to work it on their behalf. Common land became enclosed first by hurdles, and then by hedges planted to consolidate the temporary barriers. Farms became bigger and sheep grazed nigh-on everywhere it was possible to graze sheep. The hedge then was no symbol of man and nature in harmony, it was one of dispossession and change. Up in Wymondham, Robert Kett rebelled, and swathes of Norfolk's rural poor, accompanied by many from Suffolk, rose with him. They pulled up those 'damned hedges and hurdles' and followed Kett on his march to Norwich. The peasant army held the city to siege, presenting the king's representative with a paper of their twenty-nine grievances over enclosure, hedges and the swingeing agricultural changes. Kett failed, as rebels and revolutionaries tend to do in England, and he, along with 3,000 of his fellows, was put to death. The hedges stayed in place, the sheep kept grazing and the rural poor went back to being rural poor.

Despite all that, booms have a bust. This came spectacularly for Suffolk. Henry VIII's addiction to fighting continental wars halted overseas trade. Simultaneously Dutch clothiers brought in lighter-weight materials, swiftly making our heavy woollens appear as outdated as Dralon. By the seventeenth century a mere 20 per cent of Suffolk's workers were employed in the wool trade. 'King Wool's' final death rattles were the clack-clack of the northern cotton mills, and there ended Suffolk's brief fling as the wealthiest and most populated place in Britain outside of London. It took generations for Suffolk to recover from this devastating body blow, and the county recoiled back to being a mixed-agrarian, insular and self-reliant place, tucked out on the eastern arse of England, first to see the sun and almost free of visitors. After all, you don't pass through Suffolk to get anywhere. The hedgerows here fell into disrepair or were felled for firewood. 'Without sheep, who needs all of those hedges?', the locals sensibly reasoned.

The wool towns are part of a larger region covering South Suffolk and North Essex, now marketed by second-home owners flogging Airbnbs as 'Constable Country', monikered in honour of John, the landscape painter from East Bergholt. Look at his works and they bear witness to an impoverished Suffolk, brought low by the agricultural depression of 1815, which was caused by a series of poor harvests and cheap foreign food imports, possible once more now that Napoleon's navy no longer stalked the English Channel. Constable was an early realist, his scenes show rural life largely shorn of romanticism. His trees are storm-damaged or pollarded – yet the rivers run clean. The shepherds who drink from those streams are emaciated children dressed in ill-fitting and ragged clothes. Honest John's then unfashionably large brush-strokes depict glowering clouds over fields at harvest, where the stooks stand blackened by endless rain – the year 1816, at the height of Constable's pre-eminence, was known as 'the year without summer'. All of which highlights that the near-devastating challenges our farmers still face today, caused by unseasonal weather and cheap foreign imports, are merely part and parcel of the perpetual agrarian cycle. Constable rarely included a hedgerow in his works, but not through laziness or artistic licence; indeed, the attention to detail Constable lavished on the sylvan elements of his paintings was, as art historian Iris Wien notes in their essay 'The Opaque Nature of John Constable's Naturalism', 'specific and scientific'. The hedgerow is absent simply because he didn't see them. In Constable's Suffolk, the hedge was old hat, a throwback to the sixteenth century when the fields were stuffed with sheep, now largely surplus to requirements. The hedgerow seen, or not seen, on old maps or in the works of Suffolk's artists, sheds true light on the reality, mirroring the history, politics, prosperity and faddishness of farming. The hedge is in truth rarely a permanent feature; they come, they go, and they come again.

Jeremy Squirrel's farm is a rarity, or at least part of it is, because his land provides a glimpse of what the Suffolk landscape may have looked like back in those boastful late-mediaeval prosperity years – at least it does if you squint a bit. The Squirrel hedges – so hated by Kett's peasant army – went unmolested, remaining in situ. They weathered the agricultural depressions of the early nineteenth century, becoming cherished and adopted by a great Victorian called John Stevens Henslow, the village parson and mentor to Charles Darwin. The studies and observations this cleric made of the fauna and flora found in these ancient hedgerows inspired his pal to pen a book on evolution. The single Squirrel holding, as it is now, had once been two farms worked by brothers – Jeremy's grandfather and great uncle. One brother loved those old hedges, their history and heritage. He loved the birds that lived within and the partridges that flew over, a brace or two of which he'd shoot after harvest in the company of a few farming neighbours. The other brother obeyed the doctrine of the post-war Ministry of Food, largely ridding his farm of two hedges in four, doing as he was told and thereby increasing his yields to feed the masses. It is a strange phenomenon to walk where the Squirrels farm. On one side of the road to the wool towns you find a place stuck in the aspic of time, on the other a place of large arable fields, ringed with a two-metre grass margin framed with hedgerows planted in the early 2000s, a view you will find in much of this county. The Squirrels of today boast a shade under fifty kilometres of hedgerows on their 800-acre farm; 80 per cent of these are wedged into a mere 40 per cent of the land mass. The patchwork fields that the old hedges create are by today's standards tiny. For modern farming they are a hindrance, in truth a cash-sapping, bottom-line-busting pain in the bank balance. Small fields mean more turns are required when cultivating, fertilising and harvesting, and profit margins tighten. Aside from the financial implications, small fields make farming dirtier: more diesel is burned, carbon debts grow wider. It is an unassailable truth that if all England's farms looked like the archaic 40 per cent of Jeremy's land, criss-crossed with hedgerows and a gnarled old oak every hundred yards or so, then our wildlife would delight at the thought. For them there would be food in abundance, protection from predators in profusion and nesting sites as common as rain clouds in October. Yet, such farming today would be catastrophic for the general public. Production costs in these tight confines, Jeremy says, are nearly double that in his open fields. Grocery prices would soar, causing a cost-of-living crisis that few living today could imagine. Hunger, real hunger, like that which the labourers in Constable's paintings knew, would be the reality, but of course governments cannot stomach public hunger, so they would import more and yet more food from countries where environmental and welfare standards are far lower than those British farmers must adhere to. As we can see from history, the hedge only has a value to farmers, and ultimately us consumers, if it helps to produce food efficiently. Delightful, beautiful and ecologically vital as Jeremy's hedges are, they do not cost-effectively help to fill human bellies. Yet, regardless of these practical, environmental and financial truths, there remains a growing clamour in England that we must plant more hedges.

The CPRE – originally the Council for the Preservation of Rural England, then the Campaign to Protect Rural England, and now CPRE, the countryside charity – have taken up the mantle of championing our hedges; notably, they are strong supporters of the small band of professional hedgelayers. Their campaigns also include admirable efforts such as lobbying for a return of council-tenant farms, improved rural bus services, reductions in light pollution and better rural recycling facilities. The CPRE claim that we have lost 40 per cent of our hedgerows since the end of the Second World War, which may be true, but as we have seen, the English farmland hedge is forever in a state of flux. They, like me, recognise that the post-war reduction in English farmland hedgerows has been a leading factor in catastrophic biodiversity loss and associated environmental declines. The CPRE's solution to this loss was to lobby for 40 per cent more hedges to be planted across England by 2050: 'That's equivalent to 120,000 miles or halfway to the moon,' they added by way of elucidation on their website. This notion, which on the surface seems laudable, has a number of flaws.

When the CPRE began their campaign, they had no realistic idea of just how many kilometres of hedgerow there actually are in England. In 2024 the UK Centre for Ecology and Hydrology gave us the answer. They undertook a full-scale LiDAR (Light Detection and Ranging) survey of the nation's hedgerows using drones and satellites. Thanks to this, we now know there are 355,000 kilometres of hedgerows in Britain and, superfluous to any practical application, the average height of them. Sadly, however, we remain completely in the dark as to their condition. Knowing the length and height of a hedge is largely window dressing, certainly in hedgerow-management terms. The LiDAR technology failed to reveal the variety of species or identify if hedges were mere banks of bramble and failing elm sucker. More vitally, the hi-tech surveying could not and did not reveal the basal condition of hedgerows, the very place where life and rejuvenation begins, and therefore the most important aspect of the hedge, ecologically speaking. Such information can only be gleaned by getting on your feet, walking the hedgerows and identifying with a practitioner's eye its current state, and thereby the future management prescriptions that will ensure a vibrant mosaic of hedgerows across a farm. To my knowledge, Gouldy and I are currently the only professional hedgers in East Anglia who undertake these hedgerow assessments in order to create detailed management plans. While in English woodlands, the law states that both mapping and assessment must be made before any work can be undertaken within them, this is not the case for our hedgerows.

Secondly, planting new hedges is undoubtedly an admirable act, and not a bad payer if you are prepared to break your back in repetitive bending toil. However, lobbying to plant half a moon shot's worth of new hedges without first accurately assessing, measuring and then making good the old – through laying, coppicing and incremental trimming – is an act of profligacy. Following our survey of Jeremy Squirrel's farm, we gleaned he already boasts a plentiful hedgerow network; what he needed was financial support to better manage what he already has, and the people to carry out the work. Put simply, you don't build a new house just because the windows and doors on your old one need a lick of paint. Finally, there is the problem of human resources and logistics. In order to plant 193,121 kilometres of additional hedges, it would require UK tree nurseries to grow the somewhat dizzying figure of an additional 965,605,000 hedging saplings (we advocate planting five hedge whips for every metre, not the six plants as recommended by Defra). In 2024, UK nurseries succeeded in growing just over 16 per cent of this figure, and this total also comprises hardwood and softwood trees used in woodland creation and commercial forestry. Every hedge whip will require a support cane, invariably bamboo imported from China, and a plastic guard. While there are biodegradable versions of these guards available, they are on average 43 per cent more expensive than single-use plastic versions, and there is ongoing debate in the sector over their efficacy.

Obviously, hedgerows don't plant themselves. According to a 2022 report by the Institute of Chartered Foresters, there is a 78 per cent shortfall in the arboricultural workforce – the rather fancy title that we hedgers fall under. Even if we could somehow grow the necessary 36 million whips each year, additional to those already grown to supply existing demand, and import the canes, and source and supply the plastic spirals to protect them, there are woefully too few people to plant them – nor are there any plans to increase the funding for land-based colleges where the next generation of planters, hedgelayers and coppicers would be trained.

Of course, planting a hedge is, comparatively, the easy bit. The care and management of 965 million precocious young hedging plants stretching halfway to the moon is extensive. All will require mulching, irrigation and regular weed control for at least the first three years of their life, depending upon growth rate. At some point, all of the plastic guards will need to be removed and disposed of. After a decade or so the now-mature hedge will require laying if it is to maximise its potential; if left to its own devices it will need coppicing after twenty years.

In March 2023 the government announced it agreed with the CPRE, if in a somewhat scaled-back way. They revealed a commitment to plant 45,000 miles (72,420 kilometres) of new hedgerows by 2040. This may not be the moon shot that the CPRE was seeking, but it still equates to 13,411,111 new hedge whips that need to be grown, planted and cared for every year for seventeen years. I highlighted the practical flaws in this policy to Jeremy's local MP James Cartlidge. Mr Cartlidge blocked me on Twitter. I raised the issue with Thérèse Coffey, then Secretary of State for Defra, at a function celebrating rare farm-animal breeds. She smiled and changed the subject.

The CPRE is an example of many well-meaning and concerned organisations, charities and individuals who are responding to the ever-growing clamour for rapid and swingeing change to take place in the English countryside. For they understand that it is here in the Sticks that nature recovery can happen, and biodiversity losses can be plugged and reversed. Government ministers and shadow ministers and all points in between are not deaf to these calls. The voices of well-supported and highly drilled PR campaigners and lobbyists ring out loud and clear, providing often simplistic solutions to the toe-curlingly intricate problems. 'Plant more trees . . .' 'Plant more hedges . . .' they say. 'This will save the planet.' The politicians lap this up, seemingly oblivious to the practical realities. Quick-fix solutions fill the pages of manifestos and win over voters. I suppose it does keep Gouldy and me in work and maintains the steady greying of our hair.

But our solution for bringing some clarity to how to solve the national hedgerow issue was, to us, fairly obvious. If woods must first be assessed and mapped prior to management or creation, then why not hedgerows too? Our argument was to put the hedge on a par with the wood. Jeremy listened to our reasoning, and as a farmer involved in the pilot for the government's Sustainable Farming Incentive (SFI), he commissioned Gouldy and me to create a plan for his farm's hedgerows. His decision was not solely driven by his interests as a conservationist farmer, keen to ascertain the health, condition and biodiversity baseline of his hedges. This for him was a leafy version of management consultancy hybridised with a stocktake. He wanted us to make a business case for the hedgerows he already had, and to ascertain if it was either physically or financially feasible to plant any more.

Making these plans is a fairly straightforward if laborious process. We use a digital system called MySOYL, developed by the crop production and grain marketing giant Frontier. On this system a satellite map of each land parcel is revealed, the rather dull term for a field. A farmer can input various layers onto these maps. One layer may map the fields that have been limed, or fertilised with muck, or sprayed with chemicals. Over this can be laid a yield map, assessing the efficacy of these efforts, revealing if there is a return in crop yield from the inputs into the soil. The farm, as seen on MySOYL, becomes a series of layers, each revealing in clinical, digital starkness real-world uncertainties of trying to make a living from growing plants in mud. We adapted this system to work for hedges. On our satellite layer the hedgerows first appear as lines of perfect green, interspersed with the mushroom-like blobs of trees – from space, hedges appear perfect. On the ground the story is markedly imperfect, hence why it is imperative to physically walk the hedgerows. The gaps we clearly see are invisible to the eye in the sky, inevitably filled as they are by clumps of rank bramble or dog rose. A tree on a satellite image turned out, when viewed from the ground, to be a fly-tipped dumpy sack filled with builder's waste. Because of this huge difference between space life and real life, our only course for an accurate assessment is to drive and walk along the boundaries and stubbles, assessing, by eye, every metre of hedgerows we see.

We first look at the overall state of the hedge, giving each length a condition score, with H1 denoting a hedge flailed to bits, up to H10 which indicates a hedge now grown into a line of trees. We record the hedge's height and width, the ditches that run alongside the hedgerow, the plant species present, and the variations in condition along each entire length. Are there gaps? Are trees shading out the thorns below? Has the hedge slumped into the ditch thanks to the cutting bucket of the digger? What is dead, we ask, and what lives? Is there room for a new hedge to be planted, to link up habitats more effectively? We mark down extraordinary wildlife – a dormouse nest, a brood of grey partridges or turtle doves feeding nearby. We look at the terrain, historic features, and glean how the farmer farms.

This latter point is key. Hedges are doubtless wonderful things for wildlife, but they can, as was seen in 1945, be hindrances to profitable and effective farming. Some farmers see profitability as the only consideration. It is simplistic to decry these individuals as plain greedy; avarice is, after all, a driver for so much in society. How many people truly think about the biodiversity loss that their own job has caused? Does the lecturer, the loss adjustor or the lawyer incarcerated in an office lose any sleep over the old meadowland that was ripped up, the habitats lost, the species made homeless, the soil denuded under concrete footings, all to make way for the shiny construction of glass and tubular steel in which he or she works? I doubt it. Their wholly understandable primary concern is that their pay cheque comes in at the month's end and the world goes on turning. Most people are primarily driven by money, if we are honest, and earning that money, paying your bills, feeding your family, and maintaining a roof over your head trumps most other considerations. Why should farmers be any different? Creating hedges, margins, ponds and woods qualifies for grants but in the long term they do not, at present, generate meaningful or sustainable income; growing food, however, does. Some farmers may be guilty of filling in a pond or mangling a hedge so that it fails, but they are no different from the rest of us. Humans are inherently selfish animals, and other wildlife will always come second to what we see as our own immediate needs. Therefore when we plot and map and assess, then prescribe management plans for hedgerows on farms, we are not only making a case for their care so that they will work better for wildlife; the hedge, vitally, must also work for the farm. Quite simply, Jeremy may be a conservationist farmer, but he is also a businessman whose business is growing food where the margins between profit and loss are so tight that the very pips squeak.

After five days of walking, driving and note-taking around Jeremy's farm, Gouldy and I retreat to my study, the leaking structure that sticks like a double-glazed tick to the side of my cottage. We begin to turn our observations into cold, hard facts and actions. Every field on every farm in England is given a unique land-parcel number by the Rural Payments Agency. These numbers are dull things, only referred to when civil servants come sniffing about. So we also include the name by which the fields are known to the farmers. One thing that seems to remain a constant on farms, regardless of technological advances, are field names. Some of these land monikers bear the names of ploughmen long gone: Parkers and Jacks. Others are more mundane: Clay Hill and Stone Field, for example, hardly requiring Holmesian powers to decipher their origins. Jeremy's fields subscribe to both the dull and interesting schools of field naming. One in particular, called Hangdown, puzzled me as we assessed the hedgerows there. (From my notes I see our prescription reads: 'Shape up with flail and maintain for five years then review. Section in middle 30 m long, near ash tree containing sparse, going backward, elms that could be coppiced'.) Back at his yard Jeremy explained the reason why Hangdown is so called with a dark sense of pride. 'The wood behind Hangdown had an old cottage in it. The family who lived there got ergot poisoning, the last recorded case in England apparently.' He warmed to the tale, seeing my eyes widening. 'My grandfather said it turned them all mad and they were all found hanging from the rafters.' Who knows if the story is wholly or even partly true, but macabre yarns are popular things in the countryside.

The first column of our spreadsheet we create in our planning bears the RPA official number, the next the colloquial field name. After this we allocate each length of every individual hedge a unique number. Rectangular fields are a simple matter of numbering from one to four. Fields that still retain their nooks and crannies and crazy-angled corners receive umpteen numbers; the digital map begins to criss-cross with a web of coloured lines. In the accompanying spreadsheet the columns are filled with numbers, descriptions and finally the prescriptions we recommend for the maintenance or rejuvenation of each hedge-length, the costs that these will incur and the income from grants that may be recovered. These hedgerow management plans were, up until a few years ago, a project that only Gouldy and I undertook. After extensive lobbying, we persuaded Defra to include hedgerow management plans in the SFI Hedgerow Standards. It is a common-sense notion: in order to manage existing hedges, or before planting new ones, a farmer first needs to know what is there. On the day the details of the SFI were released to the public, I opened the missive from the Ministry on my email. It was a most peculiar feeling to read my own words included in a piece of government legislation. There is one final column in our hedgerow management plans down which nearly every row is filled, bearing the letters 'DD'. This stands for deer damage, and is, for the health and well-being of our farmland hedges, the antlered elephant browsing in the corner of the room.

4

Silent Jim

I park up, leaving my truck skewed across the middle of the single-track lane. There is a cyclist standing in front of me; the tight-fitting yellow shirt and black shorts he wears look garish in this tree-lined tarmac tunnel. He stares down into the roadside verge, hands to his head like a ham actor. I open the door and walk to his aid. He turns his head towards me then looks hurriedly back down to the grass. I follow his gaze. The buck has a fine head, his antlers appear buffed clean, the tines supported on a circular crown. I am no expert at ageing roe deer. I vaguely remember being told by Silent Jim that the older the buck, the deeper the coronet on which the antlers are set.

The eye appears lined with kohl, the pupil and iris are indistinguishable from each other, black and shiny. Bright with life, yet somehow unseeing. The buck thrashes, the cyclist and I move back half a step and it is then I notice the buck's body only bends from a mid-point down his spine. Behind his rib cage, the rounded haunch and spindle shanks are immobile in the ditch. Animal pain is hard to discern in some species. When my dog stands on a blackthorn barb her expression is no different from mine when I do likewise. Our brows both furrow at the throb as we hobble about. This buck is in pain, he must be in pain, his back appears broken and the offside hind cannon bone is jagged and bloody, jutting at a crazy angle. Yet he makes no groan or scream. His attractive, slightly angular face carries no hint of what he is feeling as his forequarter writhes in this ditch surrounded by cow parsley and forget-me-nots. His front end attempts to flee from the combination of unfathomable agony and his inbuilt terror of man in such close proximity. His rear end is already dead. I make a phone call, dialling 111, and speak to a woman with a monotone voice. The lone cyclist stands with me all this time, hands now fiddling with a toggle on his shorts. We wait together for what seems like an hour, during which I check and recheck my telephone, willing it to ring.

Deer are a sight of wonder. To see one brought so low is a terrible thing. 'The van was going so fast, he just drove off,' the man tells me for the fifth time. The buck sinks his shoulder back down and I stoop to keep his head steady, like I would with a horse suffering colic. My preventing him from flailing is more to find something to do than to provide any practical help. The phone rings and buzzes: an Ipswich number, I note. An inspector from Martlesham introduces himself. I describe the scene, just as I had fifteen minutes before to the woman in the emergency services call centre. The police officer asks me for a situation report and for my credentials to deal with this horror. 'Road traffic collision,' I explain. 'Broken back. Shotgun, magnum,' I assure him. 'You may proceed,' he replies. I stand up, walk to my truck and remove the ugly black Turkish semi-automatic shotgun from its slip. It has laid hidden under banks of jumpers and other assorted half-dirty, half-clean work clothes on my vehicle's back seat. The cyclist looks at me properly for the first time. His expression tells me that guns are not a part of his life. 'It's the kindest thing,' I say, sounding like a clichéd vet in a TV drama. 'Thank you for your help,' I add. He nods, mounting then wobbling off on his bike. I slide two cartridges into the magazine and finish the job started by an anonymous driver in an anonymous white van, his attention most likely on a Sat Nav, trying to locate some lost cottage within our unfathomable lattice of country roads. No doubt he was going at speed; online shoppers demand they receive their purchases within hours of their mouse click, and the driver only keeps his job if he can aid and abet this desperate need to have that thing right now.

When the buck is lying dead, a small green van appears around the bend in the lane. It slows to a stop as the driver spies my pickup-truck road block and me re-slipping my gun. I vaguely recognise him. He rehomes feral cats from his ramshackle cottage somewhere near Mellis. He joins me to look down upon the sorry carcass; flies have already begun to buzz about the buck and sup where his unseeing eye had been. I explain and he understands; he is a countryman. 'Do you want it?' he asks. I shake my head. 'All bone and blood that one.' He opens the back doors of his van and I help him to lift the roe in. His cats will have venison tonight and for a fair few more to come.

IN A RARE MOMENT of consensus, the British Association for Shooting and Conservation (BASC) and the lobbying group Rewild Britain both estimate that the British deer population is the highest it has ever been. This is no good for hedges. The British Deer Society research shows that deer need to eat approximately 10 per cent of their own body weight daily to survive. The average weight of the five species present in the UK hovers around 65 kg, meaning each and every deer drawing breath is looking to fill its rumen with over 6.5 kg of green matter each day. In lowland Britain, much of that intake is found in the hedge. With a finger held up to the wind, the national herd is guessed to be somewhere around 2 million animals. Over a third of these animals are believed to live north of Hadrian's Wall. The closest we get to certainty in deer numbers is on land where professional stalkers accompany paying punters. In such places, deer pay the bills, often better than sheep or cattle. The red deer of the Scottish Highlands or England's Westmorland are some of the best managed (most realists would say the *only* managed) deer in Britain. A royal stag there may be magnificent, but professional stalkers are deer managers first and foremost. They judge which beasts are 'going back' (stalker talk for getting on a bit in years) and are therefore more likely to become less fertile and decreasingly beneficial to the health of the herd as a whole. From 1 August through to 1 April in England (the dates are different in Scotland), the monarchs permanently exit from the ecosystem via the medium of a well-placed bullet. This is the very zenith of practical conservation; the fact that the man pulling the trigger may be paying multiples of thousands of pounds for the privilege is meanwhile the epitome of good business. Hinds are similarly culled, from 1 November through to 31 March, but because these ladies lack antlers, and are shot in the teeth of winter, they are less attractive to the paying punter, therefore have a lower commercial value and tend to be culled by professional stalkers or hungry hedgelayers.

We have red deer in East Anglia, a somewhat enigmatic herd. One of just two deer species native to these shores, the mighty red has been immortalised and countless times copied in Sir Edwin Landseer's kitsch painting *The Monarch of the Glen*. Artistic imaginings aside, Scottish reds are generally far weedier specimens than those we get in Suffolk. Ours are bulky bodied and long on the leg, well fed and content on their summer diet of wheat and barley and winter feast of greens, rather than eking a sparse living on upland heather. If I rise at dawn in high summer to exercise the dogs, it is no rare thing to see a small herd of reds, their cud-chewing heads turned inquisitively towards me as they lounge amid the wheat. Even through binoculars these giants appear more akin to cattle than deer. The herds that roam here, making cloven tracks on their time-worn routes are, to be honest, the result of introduction. The story goes that the original herd were escapees from Mary Tudor's deer park at Westhorpe; over time, these late-mediaeval beasts were joined by others released by a gentleman farmer from South Norfolk. This agrarian was a master of the Norwich Staghounds, who set free his stock some time around the ban on 'carted' stag hunting – a sort of make-believe venery involving a tame hummel (antlerless) stag being transported to a meet in a horse-drawn box. Once released, the stag was hunted by hounds. The unwitting trail layer led the mounted Field on a merry dance until, fed up with all that running about, the stag brought himself to bay in a poor pastiche of true stag hunting as seen on Exmoor and the Quantock Hills. Unlike the West Country reds, the carted stag received no coup de grâce of a gunshot to the head; he was instead somewhat unceremoniously shooed, penned and then reloaded, stiff-legged but unharmed, onto the cart to be taken back home, then turned out to graze in a paddock with the horses that a few hours earlier had galloped along in his wake. The East Anglian reds are remarkably particular in their ways, rarely ever straying from their time-worn routes. The meandering tracks they wend lead from the Euston estate then follow a line eastward to the coastal heaths and forests at Dunwich. Canny farmers choose not to argue with them and mow a path for their conga line through cover crops so that they may continue to pass through unhindered.

Our other native is the roe, a far daintier beast than the red. There is a decided feeling of the ancient about them, engendering a spirit of olde England; fossils reveal they have browsed here since at least 10,000 BC. The Anglian red, even in his new-found corpulent Englishness, feels like he is and always will be a Hibernian. A roe nibbling on summer-hedgerow hawthorn is as English as a fight at the Old Farm Derby between Ipswich and Norwich football fans. A roe buck's face adorns the painted shield informing travellers they have arrived in my home village – the other vignettes being a tractor, a pub, a wheatsheaf and a water meadow, an epigram for Mid Suffolk if ever there was one. The roe in Suffolk is a totem of our *terroir*, a part of our DNA. Roe bucks love the taste of a thorn in spring, rearing up on their hind legs to reach the greenest tips in a hedge. Likewise they take out their hatred on tree guards in high summer, braying the plastic tubes to slivers with dagger-like antlers as the testosterone flushes in the rut. When a buck marks his territory and fights with rivals, it is wholly unlike that of the bellowing bovine red cousin; with roe the battles are brief but more personal, more savage. His courtship, though, is a marathon not a sprint. I watch in voyeuristic delight as an aroused and clearly horny buck follows a doe on a trotting figure-of-eight dance. His lip is curled up, revealing a salmon-pink toothless gum. He savours the sweet scent of sex that wafts from her scant snow-white scut. The chase can go on for an hour or more. She will either succumb to his advances and stand, allowing him to mate in a brief but admirably energetic knee tremble, or at some unspoken signal tell him to wait awhile, which the lothario seems to accept in a tongue-lolling and despondent fashion. With roe, like all native wildlife, a balance must be maintained, but with these ethereal ancient animals it is done with a light hand.

There is no lighter nor more ruthless hand than Silent Jim's. Jim Allen is a deer stalker; more properly Jim is a deer manager, a targeted deer killer. Jim was unaware I had dubbed him with the prefix 'Silent' until he read an article I wrote about him. I had followed him on one evening stalk, mentally taking notes of his wraith-like armed approach to a roe buck. Whilst I stumbled over molehills and tripped on twigs that cracked like rook scarers, Jim seemed to skirt these thunderous traps. Every movement he made was fluid, unhurried yet swift, no rustle, no hustle, silent. In the moment he shot the buck, he did so with a lethality only found in those completely at one with the tools of their trade.

The chief reason for the spiralling numbers of deer in England sounds like an announcement made by a golf-club bore: the problem is the foreigners (or furriners if one is reading this in Suffolk). While our reds and our roe are native, both truly belonging here, all other deer species found in the UK are not. These *Cervidae* blow-ins were imported by man solely for the gratification of man. Ecologically speaking, they have no right to be here at all. Richard Gould once said to me in one of his bouts of truck-tailgate philosophy, 'Every mouthful of thorn plucked from the hedge, each morsel of tree shoot or sapling enjoyed by a muntjac, fallow, sika or Chinese water deer was never by rights theirs to take.' (To be fair, he maybe didn't use the words plucked and morsel, but it was a while back.) These four non-native species, particularly muntjac and fallow, are to our Suffolk landscape no less unnatural or destructive to habitats than is the modern tractor with its mounted flail mower, so often demonised by environmental campaigners.

Jim's genius lies in his total and complete understanding of English deer management. He knows wholeheartedly that our native species require considered control, meaning that a balance must be maintained because they are as much a part of our landscape as we humans. The non-natives, meanwhile, need eradicating, and if this is not possible, then there should at least be a concerted and ongoing campaign of lethal control. This isn't a contradictory notion. The deer overpopulation we suffer is not due to an overabundance of reds and roe (although in some areas of lowland Britain the roe is at hitherto unseen densities). It is due to the sheer weight in numbers of the non-native species, which put pressure on the natives for food and habitat. Hedgerows suffer just as much as, if not more than, woods from deer browsing. New shoots, flower buds and foliage are stripped. New plantings are particularly popular as the growth appears above the top of the guard. If repeatedly browsed, the plant eventually gives up, withers and dies. The sheer success of the fallow and muntjac in East Anglia has caused a nearly insurmountable imbalance in our regional deer herd.

British deer no longer have any natural predators. Human behaviours and our ever-growing population saw off the apex predatory species. The wolf and the lynx are long extinct here, solely because of us humans. The suggestion by some idealists that their reintroduction to England would address the issue of deer imbalance is attractive yet fanciful – a wolf or a lynx at large in Suffolk would be a poor lost creature, each a relic of the distant past in this modern arable country, hemmed in by villages and roads, all human hands turned against them, from cat owners to sheep farmers, walkers to stalkers. Their lives would be short and would end most likely under the wheels of a lorry on the A14, becoming pancakes of mediaeval fur to be picked over by scavenging crows and foxes. That is no end for an imported wolf. The only logical solution in maintaining the trophic levels here, as the scientists term it, is to rely upon man, the last apex predator left standing. Jim, like Gouldy, is a fine example of the efficacy of man as apex predator.

A lot of Jim's success comes from observation – before he even gets his rifle out the cabinet, he spends days considering the lie of the land. He places high seats, essentially elevated hides, in likely places for a dawn or dusk ambush. He looks for tracks and tree damage, both of which indicate that deer are present. Although not blessed with the eyes of a lynx, he has the next best thing – a high-powered scope on his rifle and a handheld thermal-imaging monocular. This latter piece of gadgetry enables him to observe as a muntjac or roe hides in cover – or, more accurately, he sees a deer-shaped electro-green blob that constitutes the view in his lens. Jim has neither the speed nor the stamina of a wolf hunting down its quarry, but he does have a rifle, or rather a number of rifles, each chosen and suited for differing species and locations. He is inarguably a more effective killer than either wolf or lynx. Jim kills from long distances and can do so multiple times without tiring. If he fails to kill, he won't starve – nor, for that matter, if he does become peckish, will he turn to killing sheep, pet goats, or cats belonging to the elderly. But deer stalkers are only any good if they actually kill deer. As an erstwhile Royal Marine, shooting deer comes easily to Jim, but, like hedgelayers, there are too few deer killers about. Deer stalkers do it for the sport, for the love of the chase and some venison for the freezer, but they invariably have working lives outside deer management; theirs is a hobby not a job. Sadly, hobbyists, however keen and proficient, will barely scratch the surface of deer overpopulation. Deer killers are scarce for a multitude of reasons. The job is poorly paid, the grants for deer control are miserly, and they only relate to woodland creation or management. Despite the government's funding of hedgerow management and planting with generous grants, there is no specific provision given to support deer control to protect hedgerows.

Too few people eat or have access to the end product of Jim's deer control. He owns a business called Wild Suffolk Venison. At his home he has erected a pristine larder where he skins and joints and processes the deer he shoots into lean, free-range meat, packaged and presented to the standard of perfection that the modern consumer insists on. He retails to restaurants, to the public online or through local butchers. He doesn't waste his time trying to sell to larger retailers – the prices supermarkets offer are laughably low, that is even if the grocery behemoths would take his product in the first place. Tesco, for example, rarely stocks wild British deer meat, disliking the complications caused by seasonality and dealing with small processors. Most supermarkets, if they sell it at all, prefer to retail farmed venison. This meat is just as likely to come from one of the 900,000 red deer commercially farmed in New Zealand. While there are no precise government figures for imported deer meat, the Scottish venison partnership estimates that 3,000 tons arrive annually in the UK from New Zealand. Jim argues that only when the shopper here can easily source and buy wild venison will the deer problem be on its way to being solved.

Jim shoots hundreds of deer each season; he has a group of like-minded killers who join him when he is called upon to undertake meaningful culls. These mass killings are militaristic in both planning and execution. Yet their effectiveness is hampered by the understandable safety considerations of using a high-powered rifle near conurbations and the simple fact that the costs don't add up. Meanwhile the hedges we plant, lay, coppice and love continue to get eaten.

Of non-native deer, sika are mercifully not yet present in Suffolk. The Chinese water deer, however, seem to get on here quite happily. Further east, on the Broadland marshes, they are a common sight, and we now see them in Mid Suffolk too, amidst the wild-bird-cover crops that butt up against the hedges we lay. Their deep, lustred eyes contrast attractively with the autumnal colours of their dense jacket, black lips curled in a permanent cheerful grin. Only the devilish fangs sported by the bucks ruin the full cartoon 'furbaby' look. They are skittish animals, panicking in blind terror should you surprise one in cover. Their diet and density hardly raises the ire of either farmer or hedgelayer; they munch on grass for the main. However, in Bedfordshire and Northamptonshire, for example, where numbers have boomed, deer managers now note that saplings are beginning to suffer from the attention of the Chinese. Their venison tastes delicious and Silent Jim offering up a prized haunch or back strap is a mark of strong friendship.

Muntjac, like Chinese water deer, are from Asia. The Duke of Bedford thought, in the way that nineteenth-century dukes did, that they might make a pleasant addition to the fauna of his park. He believed his friends would appreciate them too, so when he went a-visiting he gifted his hosts with a pair or two, much like I might with a bunch of forecourt flowers. The diminutive yet butty muntjac had no regard for being exhibited in a deer park and duly made successful bids for freedom. Since the first specimens broke out from Woburn in 1838, they have spread and bred and spread again throughout the south and east. The munty – unlike all other deer species found in Britain – has no rutting season, breeding all year round. Muntjac does are in a permanent state of either pregnancy or feeding a youngster. Bucks fight like badgers with other males, one look at the scarred shoulders and face of muntjac in the deer larder prior to skinning reveals their tusks are a savage weapon. Once a territory is established, the victorious buck leads a life of eating and regular sex. Yet the muntjac is no herd species – they live in a loose commune; neither neighbourly nor reclusive, they just rub along. The vanquished males bide their time, living in the margins waiting for when they feel sufficiently emboldened to challenge the local hardman in a fight for the ladies once more.

In the mid-1980s I went to a talk given by Richard Prior, the recognised world expert on roe. He was asked by an audience member if he thought muntjac numbers might become problematic. He replied that, in his opinion, muntjac are far too secretive and shy of man to thrive to any degree, largely due, he concluded, to human pressure in our ever increasingly built-up England. He predicted they would only ever inhabit isolated scrub blocks and thickets. Richard was rarely wrong, but he was wrong about muntjac. These unwitting incomers have become to conservationists, farmers, hedgelayers, arborists, silviculturists and nightingales, the most pestilential of creatures. A study funded by the British Trust for Ornithology (BTO) and written by Charles Holt, Robert Fuller and Paul Dolman was conducted in Bradfield Woods, near Bury St Edmunds. A correlation was noted between the simultaneous increase in the deer population within the area and a marked decline in nightingale numbers. To confirm this, eight plots were coppiced within the wood then left to rejuvenate, producing the dense understorey habitat demanded by nesting nightingales. Deer were excluded from half of each of these plots using steel Heras fencing. The deer-free zones quickly became fifteen times denser in cover than those in the browsed areas. Using radio telemetry and territory mapping of male nightingales it was shown that the birds spent 69 per cent of their time within the areas free from deer. The conclusion of the research was that deer had a strong negative impact on habitat suitability for nightingales and other bird species that require a dense understorey within woodland. Translated into non-scientific terms, if you have a high density of roe and then add an abundance of non-native muntjac to the mix, you won't have nightingales.

Scrub is a precious jewel in habitat terms. It is largely made up of blackthorn and bramble, and stunted, gnarled hawthorn often grows up among it too. The hedge is essentially the man-made version of scrub, similar in its thorniness, but while the hedgerow is a linear ribbon, scrub blocks spread to spit and spot grassy meadows. With the loss of our meadowlands, scrub is now largely only found in rough field corners, wet hollows, abandoned piggeries or on railway embankments, essentially places where crops would struggle to grow. Farmers ignore these places as unprofitable relics. Thanks to the combination of protection, food provision and the absence of man, scrub is often home to innumerable birds like the turtle dove, whitethroat, dunnock, chiffchaff and of course the nightingale. These places are full of life, yet I can count on the fingers of one hand the number of times I've heard a nightingale's moonlit serenade within a scrub block in the past two decades. How tragic and wasteful and just plain wrong that this red-listed bird species has vanished, not due to agricultural malpractice, predation, urbanisation or lack of care. No, the nightingale dwindled, then went, largely because their nesting habitat is no more, the understorey all eaten away by muntjac.

Muntjac are small: a tall one measures a mere 50 cm at the shoulder. Being low to the ground, they browse the areas where the building blocks of hedgerows, scrub and woodlands begin. Investment of time and money, toil and sweat are all for nigh-on nought when muntjac are present. Silent Jim shoots every muntjac he sees. Yet he cannot kill them all. Incomers swiftly move in to fill the gaps created by his rifle. Village-edge gardens with their attractive shrubberies provide secure housing from which they roam out. The footpaths that cross the farm make unsafe backdrops to shoot over; the cover we provide for other wildlife is cover for the munty too. The muntjac is here to stay and we must accept that unless a nationwide, concerted, costly and ruthless eradication campaign is undertaken, our hedges are at threat and nightingales will never return in parts where these deer are present.

Fallow deer are to trees what muntjac are to hedges and scrub. The incisor teeth of fallow, like all deer species, are only found on the lower jaw, which makes for a tearing action when browsing. Bucks bray trees during the rut with their palmate antlers. The damage that one fallow buck can achieve is significant; when in herds, the aftermath of a fallow visitation is akin to a destructive child piloting a JCB through your woods. The fallow were early migrants, arriving here with the Normans. A medium-sized deer, they are aristocratic looking beasts and were released into parks and deer forests, jealously protected so that the two-legged aristocrats of the day had deer to hunt and venison for the table. The bucks stand at nearly a metre tall and weigh 20 kg more than the average man. They are herd animals, and this trait is the root of the problem. Fallow are by no means thick. They have gleaned that man is an enemy, particularly a man with a rifle. Shoot one out of a parcel of four and three have learned that danger is out there. The trio move off in search of more fallow to bide with; safety, after all, lies in numbers. The herd that they join will have members within it that have also learned that a rifle bolt's click tolls danger. Before long, herds become engorged, each member fully aware of the prescient need to avoid the deer stalker. These enormous herds become almost invulnerable; the only means of control would be to lamp them at night. Our current legislation has only recently changed to permit this, and the application process is a bureaucratic nightmare. Thus the fallow continue to thrive and grow in number, browsing and thrashing their way through the trees and scrublands of England.

The 'DD' we note, in our hedgerow management plans, indicating deer damage, is as much a threat to the well-being of the hedge, and therefore the wildlife that calls it home, as the actions of an overzealous flail operator or the natural effects of drought, flood or wind rock. Browse lines, which in fairly short order cause hedges to mushroom out at the top and dwindle and fail at the bottom, are evident on nearly every hedge in East Anglia. On one recent hedgerow survey we noted that we'd lost 80 per cent of the whips in a one-and-a-half-kilometre-long new hedge. Each whip had been repeatedly browsed hard by muntjac and roe until it withered and died in its plastic guard. While the devastation this causes to biodiversity is obvious, such damage has financial implications too. The cost to the taxpayer for 1,200 metres of new hedgerow lost through this deer damage is £22,564.00 – one metre of hedge planting currently receives a grant of £22.97 from Defra. Admittedly the landowner shoulders the immediate financial cost, having to replace and replant the lost hedge whips at their own expense. Even if a meaningful cull is undertaken on one farm, deer move back into the area from neighbouring land where control is absent. Deer in the east of England have become for hedgers and woodland managers a Sisyphean trial. This raises the question: what is the point? Why should Gouldy and I scratch our arms to pieces in all weathers, planting, laying or coppicing hedgerows, to be paid by farmers, via taxpayer-funded grants, to encourage all of this habitat to bloom and grow and flush, making a home for birds, small mammals, insects, amphibians and reptiles, only for it all to ultimately disappear into the rumen of a deer that doesn't even belong here?

5

Flea Barn

I throw the square out into the sward. Four lengths of hazel wand, each one of them a metre in length, bound together at the corners by multiple wraps of Gorilla tape. It lands at a jaunty angle, held up at one corner by the sandpaper leaves of bristly ox tongue, whose flowers, a dog-bile yellow, nod at the intrusion. I crouch and kneel in the soft sand-like thatch of grasses that bend and bow under my weight. I fiddle for and then find my notebook and pencil in the map pocket of my baggy tan combat trousers and begin to list the plants within the square. It is the fifth time I have done so in this meadow; I will kneel and count five times more before I am done. The heading at the top of the page reads 'Field No. 2926'. We don't call Field No. 2926 'Field 2926'; we call it Car Park Field, because it's where we park our cars on shoot days. However, the Rural Payments Agency likes field numbers; they have no time for the vagaries and foibles of colloquial field names. 'Ribwort plantain, meadow buttercup, yarrow, white clover, knapweed . . .' – the book wobbles on my knee as I write and the blunt pencil adds to the childish quality of my writing – '. . . cow parsley'. I tap the chewed end against my bottom incisors. What is the bloody name for that hazy-pink flower? I part the grassy tangle for a better view. I know I know it and become cross at my forgetfulness. I give in and use my phone camera to take a snapshot. An app, Picture This, tells me what I thought I knew: '*Fumaria officinalis.*' Bloody Latin. My father would tell me how the prefix *Fumaria* helps the identification process, indicating the smoky appearance of the flower head. But I never did like Latin. Writing in my notebook 'common fumitory' feels like an act of rebellion. 'That's more like it, isn't it, Mabel?' She looks up from her snuffling nearby and wags her tail; any attention will do for the cocker spaniel. 'Common vetch, field buttercup, pink campion.' Now some yellow thing; my teeth receive another pencil battue. I know this one too. The flower is gorse-like. It's not gorse – I know gorse. The leaves are akin to thyme. It's not thyme – I know thyme. As larks sing overhead in a sky that is as cloudless and empty as my mind right now, I ask the dog for help. She wanders over, head lowered, stump wagging again, and nudges my hand for me to stroke her. This sends the pad and pencil tumbling into the thatch of green. The notebook is caught by the fronds, the pencil, pilfered from my son's school bag, disappears. 'Eggs and bacon,' I tell her with delight at this sudden dawning. My memory in middle age is a curious thing. It is as if I have to leaf through an encyclopaedia: slower than Google but so much more rewarding when I find the answer to a question. I see the glint of the metal pencil top and extract it from the midst of some cocksfoot. I scribble down the better-known common name, bird's-foot trefoil, and underline it in emphasis. 'Thank you, Mabel.' The little dog's head is covered in sticky green spheres, glued to the wispy tuft she sports between her eyes. Botanists would call them *Galium aparine*, I call them cleavers, and in to the book they go. 'Ha,' I say to the dog, and to the bees, hoverflies and skylarks. Mabel has already wandered off, and lies down to pant, only moving to lie next to me when I roll onto my back for a nap, staring up into the blue, framed by the waving fronds of grass.

We know that the hedgerow is essential to farm wildlife for food, habitat and nesting. We know too that the condition of our hedgerow network is largely elusive. To claim we have 'lost' our hedges is an attractively elegiac idea. Yet history shows us that they are and always were in truth a transient landscape feature, coming and going with the winds of farming change and consumer need. Meadowland has also suffered the same spasmodic disappearances and reappearances as hedgerows in Suffolk. Mark Bailey, Professor of Late Medieval History at the University of East Anglia, notes that by AD 1300 one half of the county's land mass was under the plough, thanks to the high prices then of wheat, barley, rye and oats. Grassland only returned as a staple of the East Anglian landscape in the wake of the wool boom a century and a half later. The wheel turned again at the end of the Second World War. By comparing current Rural Payments Agency land-use data and farm maps dating back to the mid-nineteenth century, it is now easy to calculate that some 90 per cent of the county's meadowland has been ploughed up since 1945. Simply using your own eyes backs up these dry statistics. When driving along nearly any Suffolk lane today, the sight of cattle grazing in water meadows or sheep nibbling on species-rich tussocky swards, enclosed by thick multi-species hedgerows, is a vision sufficiently rare to induce you to pull up in the gateway and revel at the scene. This is important, because however wonderful a hedgerow may be for wildlife, without an accompanying grassy bank or margin, rich with tussock grasses clambering up into its dense fronds, it is limited in its ability to improve biodiversity. The pollen- and nectar-rich flowers, the grasses and sedges of the meadow that butt up to a hedge, make the sum of the whole. It is here, I believe, in the margins where the battle for nature recovery can truly be won.

Flea Barn is about half an hour's drive from my cottage. As the crow flies it's not so far, but Suffolk roads shun the notion of straight lines, and the meandering route I take to get there is as eccentric and complicated as the people who live here. You won't find the name Flea Barn on a map. Like most landownership, death causes shifts and readjustments. The original Park Farm holding, as it was known, was divided as part of probate, following the passing of a maternal grandfather, and one farm became two. A pair of cousins work the land here; a concrete track is all that acts as the boundary. Will, on the south-eastern side of the hard drive, farms traditionally, his crop yield is high, his hedges are gappy. On the north-western side, towards Debenham, Will's cousin Ed farms. Flea Barn is his manor, named after a decrepit brick building, now roofless after Storm Eunice whipped off the wriggly tin like a sheaf of foolscap. A similarly driven farmer as his cousin, Ed Nesling made a decision to change his practices, not so dramatic as to go organic or rewild, add beavers and exotic fauna, but by sustainable tweaks and alterations.

Ed and I first met when he came to a talk I gave on hedgelaying. We hit it off and he invited me over to visit. We walked his farm and talked about the future of agriculture, of grants, of hedges, insects, and the end of BPS – the EU's Basic Payment Scheme, part of the Common Agricultural Policy (CAP), designed originally to assist continental farmers in post-war Europe rather than East Anglian arable growers of today. We agreed that we were embroiled in yet another agricultural revolution, and Ed chose to be a part of it. His aim was straightforward. He wanted to continue farming the land that was economically viable but sought to turn areas that were inefficient into habitat and food sources that maximise their potential for wildlife.

There is no sense in charging blindly into farm-wide

conservation projects without first creating a plan or fully understanding your natural baseline. Baseline surveying was therefore essential. Any change to agricultural practice is not without financial risk and can have long-lasting negative impacts on how you are able to farm in the future. Newly planted woods or hedges, for example, are not features that can be merely grubbed up or forgotten about if at a later date they are discovered to be in the wrong place. Additionally, if Ed failed and his farm became a sea of weeds and patchy crops, he faced no little ridicule from his peers. Ed is regarded as something of a hero among his neighbours. He is a very effective operator. And there was another looming spectre – the Rural Payments Agency. If we failed to dovetail the farming and the environmental endeavours, the RPA, who seem to delight in imposing draconian penalties on farmers, have an array of fines they can impose on landowners whom they claim have infringed the arcanely precise prescriptions of the Countryside Stewardship grants. Most of our habitat improvement would be at least part funded by a system called a Mid-Tier stewardship scheme. Stewardship essentially offers a financial incentive to recompense farmers who remove land from cultivation and turn it over to anything from new woodland to wetlands to crops that provide seed or cover for farmland birds and wildlife. Defra dangles the carrots; the RPA carries the stick.

We assessed the farm's hedgerows, and we counted the farmland birds. We looked at sites for new woods and surveyed the existing ones. Ponds were dipped, insects counted, moths trapped. And then we turned to the grassland. Car Park Field was a good case study for baseline surveying. It had not been farmed for many a year. Ed thinks twenty may have passed since this was last under the plough. It had reverted back to grassland under the set-aside scheme that was introduced by the EEC in 1988 and became compulsory in 1992 for larger arable farmers. The set-aside initiative was designed to tackle over-production and the resulting costly surpluses, and to deliver some environmental benefits where the intensification of agriculture was damaging the agricultural ecosystem and wildlife; farmers were paid to take a proportion of their land out of production, to be left fallow or to be used for other purposes such as creating woodland.

The meadows at Flea Barn comprise some fifteen hectares of the total holding and are unlike grasslands found on mixed farms. This land has long forgotten what it is to be fertilised and grazed by the cattle that Ed's grandfather once kept here. Gone are the micro flora and fauna that the cowpats once provided, the sward base no longer opened up through the lick, grip and tug of a cow's tongue. This absence is wholly a negative for meadowland. Grass itself is precocious, and begins to rule the roost, helped by the fertility of our strong Suffolk clay. The only herbage that stands up to this grassy dictatorship are the broadleaf plants such as dock and thistle. The parasol-like leaves shade out the more delicate, lower-growing wildflowers. Admittedly in spring, before the grass gets away, Car Park Field becomes a smear of dusky yellow – a carpet of cowslip, and rarer oxlip, grows in the bottom of the northern boundary hedge. This is followed by sprays of cow parsley, through which we mow paths; these act as feed rides for the turtle doves when they arrive in May and as trackways for farm vehicles. In this particular grass-checked zone, bee and pyramid orchids wave in the breeze and sunlight of mid-June. But in the uncut swards the grasses begin to dominate, the wildflowers struggle; starved of light and space, they wither, failing to flower or bear seed.

In a field grazed by cows, their actions check the dominance of these tall grasses and the broadleaf weeds. The cloven hoof scuffles up the understorey, effectively harrowing out much of the thatching, while the weight of the beasts rolls the land; it's the grassland equivalent of thinning a wood. In effect, a herd of cows can naturally create a flower-rich meadow far more effectively than any tractor can. The cattle top it, harrow it, roll it and fertilise it; it just seems that their burps are considered by a few loud voices to be more abhorrent than diesel exhaust. On some estates and reserves where a 'rewilding model' is adopted, all manner of bovines have been drafted in to improve grasslands. White Park Cattle, stumpy Dexters, shaggy Highlands and even non-native water buffalo graze the grass and bring life to the swards. And why not? Reserves are not real life, not like farming; reserve wardens can play at God and regardless of the breed they choose, cows are honest; they get their head down and take the rough with the smooth, chewing cud and little realising they are a very tasty conservation tool.

Sheep are good mowers too. Send them in as the spring sunshine warms the ground, and the meadow will burst back into life, wildflowers rearing their budding heads over the shorn grasses. They suit Flea Barn. After all, Debenham, the largest village nearby, was once a wool town. Although decried by those who advocate veganism, sheep, whether mob grazed in sharp bursts or grazed over lengthier periods in balanced numbers, are the very things to create and maintain the bucolic East Anglian meadow. Dominic, a young farmer from down the road, near Eye, ran his sheep on the grasslands of Flea Barn. It was a fair exchange really, and a model that is becoming more prevalent for new entrants to the industry. This 'grazier model' provides a win-win service for farmers like Ed. It reduces the fuel and machinery costs of topping the meadows, improves wildlife habitat, and, in return, it provides valuable grazing land for young shepherds for no rental charge. However, such entrepreneurs are too thin on the ground. Barclays bank estimates agriculture is facing a recruitment crisis, with just 3 per cent of the UK's population under the age of thirty considering farming as a career. Little wonder. The sheer hard graft, and spiralling costs of feed, and of transporting the animals to fresh pastures or the abattoir, cause ever narrowing profit margins, ensuring that a life lived as a grazier is a particularly precarious one.

Livestock, Ed admits, is 'not my business'. Farming in Suffolk has seen dramatic change since the war, with specialisation becoming the norm. Mixed farms, those with a balance of both arable and livestock interests, have dwindled to rarity status. The reasons for this are clear. For the cattle men, their stock is at constant threat of badger-borne TB, the costs of milk production are barely covered by the price supermarkets are prepared to pay, and beef prices are invariably undercut by South American imports. Sheep, meanwhile, are hard labour personified; if one is successful in preventing them from committing suicide, their fleece is worthless, costing more to shear than the price paid for the wool. As for the lamb, delicious as British meat is, a New Zealander can always undercut a UK farmer. And the British meat market is under attack not only financially but also spiritually. This latter onslaught is led most eloquently by the journalist George Monbiot, whose artful cherry-picking of science seeks to persuade consumers that the sheep is a woolly version of Napalm – 'sheep-wrecked' is his favoured phrase. On his website, Monbiot has declared that 'sheep are a fully automated system for environmental destruction', a sweeping statement that reveals much about the man, not least his misunderstanding about what is needed to make a meadow.

Little wonder then that Ed, like most farmers in Mid Suffolk, sticks to his guns as solely an arable grower. Since 1945 there has been a 77 per cent decline in farm labour, a direct result of specialisation and mechanisation. Modern arable farming can only be cost effective if the staff payroll is as low as you can make it; machinery power has replaced manpower. Ed, bar the hectic time of harvest, farms single-handedly. His is a lonely business, one of long hours spent in the isolation of a tractor cab. The only interactions he has are with the contacts on his mobile phone or the wildlife on the farm. The idyll of the mixed farm is a delight, and it is an agricultural system that is doubtless better for wildlife, but both market and social forces increasingly make it an unrealistic option, certainly in the form that Ed's forefathers understood it. In his grandfather's day hedges were much more commonplace, the finest form of stock-proofing medium. The notable strain of Suffolk Punch horses Ed's grandfather bred also needed the hedge. The old man's diaries reveal he made a healthy profit from selling his youngstock at market as well as trained animals to other farms, and notably one stallion to the Ipswich fertiliser manufacturer Fisons. Like cattle, horses need hedges as a shelter from the rain or as a parasol from the sun. The crisscross of hedgerows seen on the mixed farms were impeccably maintained, thanks to the weight of manpower then employed. These fascinating diaries, dating from 1901 to 1924, reveal the sheer number of men who were then on the payroll, men who, once the harvest was in, the hay made and the straw ricked, would sharpen their billhooks and slashers, heft a croom* on their shoulder, and set out to lay, coppice or gap up those hedgerows so vital to the well-being of the farm. It is perhaps an uncomfortable truth for those who wish to see a dramatic reduction in, or even wholesale cessation of, livestock farming, that not only have our meadowlands suffered from the loss of cattle and sheep, but so have our hedgerows. Put simply, in much of arable country the hedge is somewhat redundant, and anyway, there are all too few people now working the land to effectively manage them to the degree Ed's grandfather knew.

In my meadowland baseline survey here at Car Park Field, I count and record the plants and grasses found within that metre square thrown out onto the sward. I repeat this ten times in one acre, using my home-made device crafted from hedging binders. I am not primarily looking for rare species, however delightful they may be when I discover them. The purpose of the initial

---

* A croom looks like a muck fork with five prongs angled at forty-five degrees; it is used to rake up the brash created by hedge cutting.

survey is to see what is there at ground zero. Ongoing analysis will then assess the efficacy of our meadowland renovation efforts, providing a before-and-after view.

Luckily, Ed is very adept at growing plants, and, like farmers of old, is something of an innovator. He used a disc drill, a device that enables farmers to sow without ploughing, to introduce wildflower seed into the existing meadow. His reckoning was that if the grass was first topped tight by a mower, the hay removed, then immediately seeded with a mix of native wildflower species, the germinating seedlings would thrust their way up and get ahead of the smothering grasses, thereby enriching the whole. By including the plant yellow rattle in the seed mix, we hoped that the parasitic effect the plant has on grasses would check their growth and provide more space for wildflowers. But innovation does not guarantee success, or certainly not in the way one always hopes. In 2019 we put Ed's plan into action. Immediately after sowing, the weather turned dry against expectation. The drills he created baked hard into crumbling lines. The sown seed desiccated, achieving less than 10 per cent germination. However, where the claw of the drill had passed, older seed, seed that had lain dormant for decades, was awoken from its stasis and erupted into life. Fumitory, lady's bedstraw, hop trefoil and lesser bindweed appeared where none had been seen before. The mower and the drill acted in the way of cattle, agitating the soil and exposing old seed beds. The longevity of dormant seed is indeed remarkable, arguably best highlighted by the experiments carried out by the American botanist William James Beal that began in 1879. Beal buried twenty capsules filled with seeds. He dug one up every five years and sowed the seeds within to check their viability. The last of his capsules was unearthed in 2021 (unsurprisingly Beal wasn't present, having died in 1924). Incredibly two of the seed species within still germinated readily.

The most pertinent Defra grant available under stewardship for maintaining meadows such as Car Park Field is 'GS2:

Permanent grassland with very low inputs'. GS2 pays a mere £151/ha/annum, barely enough to cover the diesel when it can be mown. If the existing meadows at Flea Barn were entered into GS2 it would prohibit many of the management practices that Ed utilises, such as grazing and topping. So his decision was to keep all of the old meadowland at Flea Barn out of stewardship; it allowed him the freedom to manage it for wildlife his way, negating the stifling stipulations of Defra or a visitation by the dreaded Rural Payments Agency. It does, however, mean that these fifteen hectares of land don't make Ed any money. For some farmers this is something that would never be permitted. Farms are businesses, after all. Why leave land, they argue, to go to 'waste' when it could be making a financial return? Hence under the plough the old grasslands went, and with them their biodiversity. This is a truth that seems lost on individuals who seek to solely blame farmers for biodiversity loss. Some highlight the wildlife they see in nature reserves and ask why things are so different on farmland. There is a false equivalence that farmers and NGOs – the RSPB and Wildlife Trusts – are somehow comparable. The NGOs have a remit to improve the lot of wildlife and maintain reserves upon which that wildlife lives. These organisations, like farmers, can and do apply for Defra stewardship grants to improve land for wildlife. In some circumstances the charities can also generate income through farming. The RSPB, for example, owns such a holding, Hope Farm in Cambridgeshire, where for twenty years they have endeavoured to farm in a nature-friendly manner. But unlike professional farmers, enterprises such as the model Hope Farm, or the fenced-in man-made reserve at Minsmere on the coast, are able to fill in the financial gaps and avoid the vagaries of the market through funding from donors. Whether the money comes in by shaking a bucket outside Tesco or from large lumps bequeathed by wealthy benefactors or trusts, this is a fiscal safety net that farmers can only dream of.

There is, in Britain, a perception that all farmers are 'rich blokes', who could, if they chose, fund nature recovery via their own swollen coffers, the notion being presumably that land ownership is an indicator of prosperity. Whether a farmer owns 1,000 hectares or a hundred, it does not follow that he – or she – is rich. Whatever the size of the farm (admittedly economies of scale do tend to make larger farms more profitable), a farmer only earns his or her living by making the land work – for the farmer there are no donors, no trust funds, no well-known figures making a TV appeal for financial support. According to research by the University of Reading, farming is financially in the worst place it's been in thirty years; for some sectors, particularly in the uplands, it is in a similar parlous state to that seen in the great agricultural crash of the 1930s. Farmers don't find a few million quid down the back of their tractor seat with which to rewild half their land or dig ponds, lay hedges and recreate species-rich meadows. The general public are largely unaware of agricultural economics. Wider society is similarly blind as to where food actually comes from. Research in 2024 carried out by the pie-makers Ginsters revealed that 1.4 million Britons think onions grow on trees; one fifth, the survey showed, have never personally grown anything from seed to harvest. This food ignorance leads to huge swathes of the country's shoppers being blissfully unaware of the negative environmental impacts the cheap food they buy in supermarkets have – the 45p loaves, 330g of bacon for £1.45 and four chicken breasts for less than a fiver; all of this bargain food may be good for household budgets but it is a disaster for wildlife. The cheaper our food becomes at the point of sale, the greater the pressure grows for farmers to grow food for less. Achieving this inevitably increases reliance on chemicals and decreases focus on habitat creation and maintenance. Once the Basic Payment Scheme (BPS) disappears, in 2030, this fact will become even more stark; no longer will farmers be paid to own land, removing 25 per cent off the bottom line in one fell swoop, therefore they must make as much of it work for them as possible. Yes, they could sell their farms and cash in. One hectare of Grade A arable land can set you back as much as £20,000 in Suffolk, but someone will still have to grow the food that feeds the populace.

There are those who have decided to buck this notion of making a living from cultivating the land and have 'rewilded' large swathes. Rather than growing food, they have allowed the land to do its own thing. These landowners are invariably rich, not from farming, but from external sources. Paul Lister, the heir to the MFI fortune, owns 23,000 acres of 'wilderness reserve' at Alladale in the Highlands; the richest man in Scotland, clothing retailer Anders Polvsen has rewilded 80,000 hectares. This pattern of millionaires purchasing agricultural land to 'rewild' is highlighted by Will Matthews, a senior staffer at Knight Frank, who wrote in the land agent's 2021 annual review, 'I've had three A-list Hollywood film stars get in touch this year because they want to buy an English farm and rewild it.' Rewilding seems to me akin to owning a string of racehorses or a super-yacht, a vanity, a preserve of the fabulously rich. It was Monty Don, that most middle-class and gentle of voices, who took to print to point out his concerns for the trend. In a *Times* article he wrote: 'I have a great reservation about the concept of rewilding. To make it possible you need thousands of acres and a private income, otherwise it doesn't make any kind of sense.'

Perhaps the most well-known rewilding experiment in England is at Knepp, in Sussex, where Sir Charles Burrell and Isabella Tree have turned their 1,400 hectares into what has become a nature reserve. Instead of seeking a return from growing food, at Knepp they essentially farm people. Paying guests fork out cash to stay in yurts or converted former farm-workers' cottages. In the farm shop visitors buy organic honey and meat sourced from the free-roaming pigs and cattle, as well as red deer and fallow venison. There are tours of the 'wilderness' to watch deer,

Exmoor ponies and imported storks. These altruistic rewilders are lauded as land healers, with some justification. But more wholescale rewilding of farms and estates would be a disaster for our own national food security. It is a business model that is unsustainable; while one Knepp in a county may make a living from its farm shop and tourism, there is no place for multiple Knepps in Sussex.

Regardless of the politics, it is beyond question that since the end of the Second World War vast swathes of our English meadowlands have been lost, which means that the hedgerows running alongside them are less beneficial for wildlife. These little tragedies are largely due to the ending of mixed farming, which was influenced by changes in agricultural practices driven by the CAP, and market forces obligated by the glowering dominance of the supermarkets. The net result is a near-catastrophic decline of habitat and food sources for hundreds of animal species, from barn owls to butterflies, invertebrates to reptiles, not to mention the loss of the flora itself. Rational minds understood that there had to be a balance found somewhere between farming and halting, then reversing, the loss of place for wildlife. This is what Countryside Stewardship was designed to do, and now ELMs – the government's post-Brexit Environmental Land Management schemes – are purported to refine.

Ed's solution to the loss of his grasslands and the degeneration of his hedgerows was to access the grants that best suited his wholly arable farm. The hedgerow regeneration was fairly straightforward. Gouldy and I carried out a hedgerow management plan and then put it into practice. For the meadows, Ed utilised a largely untapped resource on the farm. His system recaptures the land mosaics that were seen in the mixed farming of old, yet work within a modern arable farming system. Ed was able to more than double the meadowland on his farm, bringing back flowers and grasses that seethe and buzz and hum with pollinators and invertebrates. Rather than rewilding and removing one or more arable fields from production – the very thing that makes him his living – he achieved his ecological success in the margins.

Margins are, in laymen's terms, the green bits that surround arable fields. They are generally grass-rich strips, buffers that lie in between the edge of the cropped area and the hedge: they are the 'edges'. On some farms these have been lost in order to eke out yet more yield, with ploughing and drilling going right up to the ditch or hedge. But at Flea Barn, Ed had already retained four-metre-wide ribbons of unimproved grass around his fields. The wildflowers that naturally occurred there had done what wildflowers do, and self-seeded. The original margins had a practical role, acting as occasional roadways for farm vehicles to access fields during harvest, at drilling time or when applying sprays or fertiliser. Yet these existing grass margins were already something of a nature reserve, only rarely disturbed and largely free from the pesticides, fungicides and fertilisers that were applied to the crops growing in-field. We focused on improving the hedgerows alongside these existing margins, conservation-laying one and a half kilometres, Midland-style laying a further 500 metres of the scrubby edges around the main wood, gapped up 800 metres with new whips, and made changes to the cutting regime on the rest, shaping them incrementally with a flail into an 'A' shape, exposing more of the surface area to the sun.

A bird's eye view of Flea Barn, prior to our starting this conservation project, was one of a small central wood surrounded by meadows, including Car Park Field, and seven large, irregularly shaped arable fields growing a rotation of beans, wheat and oilseed rape. Bordering each field ran thin ribbons of grass, with largely gappy hedges punctuated by a few trees. This is the somewhat standard landscape that modern arable farming creates, and it is a cost-effective landscape at that. It was a picture we wanted to change.

The economics of conventional arable farming is fairly simple. There are inputs – the costs associated with seed, fertiliser, fuel, labour, pesticides, herbicides and fungicides – that go into growing a crop. Then there is the output, the physical crop, or crops, from which a profit is hopefully made (and out of which the farmer's salary comes). If you can keep a tight grip on, or decrease, your inputs without negatively impacting the yield of your crop, the better the gross margin and therefore the profit you make per tonne. Back when the price of diesel, fertilisers and chemicals was low, the profits that could be made from arable and vegetable crops were very attractive; add to this a guaranteed income via the BPS and things were quite rosy. Arable farming, while never a licence to print money, was arguably the best way of earning a living from the soil in most of East Anglia, hence why the old meadowland was ploughed up, the livestock sold off and cereals, oilseed and legumes now grow where cattle once grazed. However, inputs are no longer the cheap commodities they were – Putin's war against Ukraine and ongoing unrest in the Middle East have led to spiralling fuel and fertiliser costs. Between 2021 and 2023 these rises quadrupled. The price of the chemicals which had seen off agricultural pests and diseases similarly rocketed, while many of their active ingredients, so effective at ending the lives of flea beetles and weevils, were banned in order to protect other invertebrates, pollinators and water systems. Decades of artificial fertiliser, pesticide and herbicide use also began to take their toll: chemical farming eventually saps the soil, meaning that the only way one can grow a meaningful crop is to continually increase inputs. If it pays to reduce as much as possible the amount of input required to grow crops, this obviously helps environmentally too. Every time a tractor has to make a turn it sucks yet more fuel; a three-point turn triples the cost. Sprayers, their tanks filled with chemist's concoctions, become unprofitable when they are waltzing around in fields that are shaped like the Isle of Wight. Combine harvesters have become monsters that can scarcely fit into these isthmuses of land, formed in the times when the man cutting the corn was one-horse powered. The financially sensible option, therefore, was for Ed to remove these odd angles and lumps and hollows.

Ed changed the shape of his farm. He squared off the awkward corners around the field edges, taking them out of production. He sowed these now non-cropped areas with cocksfoot and Timothy grass, oxeye daisy, knapweed and cornflower. They bled into the existing four-metre grass margins, becoming swathes, widening and narrowing, following those old unprofitable, diesel-sucking contours, leaving a more economic rectangle in the middle for the crop. In some places these new margins are twenty metres wide and over one kilometre long: linear meadows appeared, running alongside the arable. Obviously, although this squaring of fields reduced inputs, it also reduced the cropped area, meaning yields were lower. The financial sting of losing yield is in part alleviated by Countryside Stewardship. Stewardship grants are paid by the government to farmers who take land out of crop production and replace it with environmentally and wildlife-friendly leys, drillings and features. One example of this is the 'AB8: Flower-rich margins and plots' grant. (Sadly, stewardship grants are generally widely known in farming circles by unromantic letters and numbers rather than the glories of herbage, seed and flower that they bring, but brevity helps when one is filling in the endless online forms that accompany any grant application!)

The AB8 grant amounts to £673/ha/annum. To put this into perspective: the average English wheat yield per hectare in 2023 was 8.1 tonnes; one tonne of feed wheat averaged a sale price around £190 in that year. It is therefore obvious that stewardship grants are not a path to easy riches. But, once established, they are guaranteed money with significantly lower input requirements. The stewardship grants for managing existing hedges are more generous. Under stewardship, the BN5 grant for hedgelaying currently pays £13.25 per metre, with a supplement of £5.82 per metre for staking and top binding. The other grants available for hedging are the 'BN6: Hedgerow Coppicing', which pays £5.33 per metre, and 'BN7: Gapping Up', paying £17.22 per metre. However, Ed has no spare time to lay, coppice or gap up his own hedgerows, being too busy farming a thousand acres solo. Therefore he passes this grant income from BN5, BN6 and BN7 on to Gouldy and me, his hedging contractors. My business is largely reliant upon two factors. First, meaningful Defra grants that are sufficiently generous to outpace inflation and pay us a living wage. Second, and arguably more importantly, we need the goodwill and support of landowners like Ed, who manage their farms with wildlife in mind, fully aware that the stewardship grants on offer bring significantly lower financial returns than if they worked every inch of their soil. It is little wonder, then, that thousands of English farmers who have embraced a more nature-friendly farming model share a sense of wounded indignation when they are so regularly and publicly accused of wholesale greed and insouciance by environmental NGOs and commentators.

Ed managed his existing grass margins by mowing a strip, one topper-width wide, through the middle. This provided 'drying ground' essential for grey partridge chicks, and the tightly clipped swards favoured feeding turtle doves. The flower-rich strips ran alongside hedges, which were in rotation, rejuvenated and improved by Gouldy and me laying or coppicing them. I would argue that here is the hedge's most overlooked asset for wildlife – the low, marginal area where the dense, thorny, hedge-shrub layers meet the grasses of the margin. The tussocks and the assortment of campion, meadowsweet, cornflower and nettle found in the immediate hedge lee provide the nesting habitat for the grey partridge and yellowhammer. Here is where the bumblebees buzz, spiders and beetles scuttle, harvest mice and dormice scale the herbage to reach the hedge itself. The grasses and wildflowers use the hedge as a scrambling net, weaving through the thorn, becoming a greater sum of many parts. This happy harmony is only possible thanks to hedgelaying or coppicing, which creates the dense, low, thorny layer, and rotational management, by mowing or grazing, of the wildflower-rich grass margins. In autumn after nesting time, Ed mowed the majority of his margins; this allowed for new growth in the following spring, whilst the portions left uncut provided a winter refuge for wildlife.

In effect, this repeating pattern of an improved margin with a well-managed thick hedge on one side essentially re-created meadows, albeit linear ones. However, unlike a traditional meadow, these margin habitats provide more edges, and it is in the edge where farmland wildlife dwells most readily in arable country. Ed's system made meandering rivers of habitat and food flowing through his farm, linking together the feature nodes of woods, scrub, ponds and long-established meadows, such as Car Park Field.

The Flea Barn margins began to show their worth with notable speed. Sward analysis, identical to what I undertook in Car Park Field, was carried out on the field edges. Sweep netting revealed that in under two years since the AB8 was sown, there was a doubling in numbers of beneficial insects. Grey partridges nested in the hedge-side tussocks. Each spring we counted our pairs; in three years they rose from four, to seven, then to fifteen. The wild pheasants made their nests in the fronds of the old grass margins, the hens fed in the AB8. New ponds were dug and old ponds were rejuvenated, sited at the end of these margin and hedge combinations, which now also had swathes of wild-bird seed and cover crops sown alongside. This linear form of wildlife-friendly farming may not have the bucolic appeal of small fields and mixed agriculture; its appearance would be alien to Ed's grandfather. Yet, does wildlife care about appearances?

In an ideal world, the great fields of our arable country would return to smaller, hedge-lined fields. Rotations would include leys of red and white clover and vetch. Stubble fallows would be commonplace, mixed farming would return, chemicals would not be used and livestock would graze in meadows. However, as in all things in life, the ideal is not a practical reality for many. The rotations of old are gone because they were costly in labour and time, poor in yield and therefore unprofitable and inefficient, incapable of producing sufficient food at a cost that today's retailers demand. Flea Barn is such a fascinating case study because it shows a middle way is possible. What this combination of hedges, edges, wetlands and woods – be they improved or newly created, and then managed to maximise their biodiversity potential – produce for nature is extraordinary.

Meanwhile, inside the ecological framework created by these hedgerows and margins, the business of arable farming can continue sustainably and efficiently. Ed is by no means organic. He applies nitrates and sprays when needed. Yet the roots of the hedges and margin flora help to filter any chemical excess, meaning the ditches run with clean water which in turn runs into ponds dug for wildlife. This hedgerow/margin filtration theory was proved at Lodge Farm, Westhorpe, home to the cousins Patrick and Brian Barker. Brian carried out a year-long water test on a number of the main ditches that crossed his farm. It became apparent that Lodge Farm's combination of wide floristic margins and well-managed hedgerows – bordering traditionally farmed arable – dramatically reduced nitrate run-off. So clean was this surface water that Anglian Water paid the Barkers a premium, based on the company's now reduced costs in the filtration processes necessary to produce drinking water. Ed, meanwhile, discovered his pesticide use, and therefore costs, decreased because the margins now contained a higher proportion of insects, such as hoverflies and ladybirds, that pre-date agricultural pests. His fuel costs and soil compaction were lessened because farm vehicles could now work the squared-off fields with greater efficiency.

So much for the edges. Flea Barn also provided a home for wildlife within the heart of its huge fields. The scheme for infield plots at Flea Barn was a meeting of minds between Ed and an ecologist called Sarah Brockless. I have a hedgelayer's suspicion of ecologists, particularly since Gouldy and I met the pair from the water company in that Suffolk wood. As with all things, generalisations hold a grain of truth, but are never absolute and tend to be largely yokel prejudice. Sarah is no 'bobble hat', more a pragmatist. She identified that Flea Barn's 172 hectares of arable land was split into a mere seven fields. Once squared off by improved margin 'meadows' and edged with healthy hedges and vibrant cover crops, the arable acres were more profitable thanks to the reduction in inputs, with any financial losses in output recompensed, more or less, by the stewardship grants. The largest field on the farm is called Mickfield Road (rather mundanely because it runs alongside the road to Mickfield). Sarah wanted to split this giant into three with new-planted hedges, an idea that had Ed mouthing 'no' within seconds. She compromised, recommending that rather than making these divisions with hedges, why not create beetle banks?

A beetle bank is a linear ridge made by repeatedly ploughing up two furrows so that a mound of earth is created, some half a metre higher than the rest of the soil around it. This two-metre wide and one-kilometre-long ridge is then sown with tussock species, to which Ed added a mix of annual wildflower seed. The grasses and flowers knit the bank together, recreating a habitat similar to that found in a hedge and grass margin. Alongside one of the beetle banks, Ed sowed a twenty-six-metre-wide block (the width of his sprayer's boom) of semi-permanent wild-bird cover, known as AB9. Next to the other bank, Sarah proposed that a lapwing plot and parcel of AB8 should be sited.

If Ed had planted a new hedge rather than create beetle banks here, it would have set this field in aspic, removing his ability to drain or alter the usage of the land parcel more or less indefinitely. Despite popular public misconception, hedges on agricultural land are afforded significant protection under law. They are 'permanent features', meaning that once one is planted, both the Wildlife and Countryside Act (1981) and the Management of Hedgerows Regulation (2024) prohibits their removal, unless the local planning authority gives permission. Such permissions are rarely, if ever, granted – certainly for agricultural purposes anyway, despite what you may read on Twitter. Building developers, meanwhile, are invariably given such licence, provided they replant a hedgerow, increased in length by a factor of 10 per cent over that of the old one. While this may sound on the surface like a fair compromise, this new hedgerow can be planted in any place of the developer's choosing and there are no regulations to govern how that hedge is managed, if at all, in the future. A beetle bank, therefore, in such large arable land parcels provides a meaningful and biodiverse linear habitat that swiftly becomes rich in pollinators, predatory insects and small mammals, and an ideal nesting habitat for grey partridge, with the added benefit that the banks are all tucked away from the questing snouts of badgers, foxes and stoats within the midst of a growing crop.

Alongside the eastern beetle bank on Mickfield Road, Ed drilled a cover crop, boringly known in the letters and numbers world of Defra as AB9. This is a bespoke blend of plants and grasses that provide cover from avian predators, and year-round food sources for an array of farmland birds. The voles, shrews and field mice that benefit from this bank-and-block combination are a boon for the resident raptor species, which in turn lessens the threat they pose to the red-listed ground-nesting grey partridges and lapwings. The beetle banks are now one of the best places to see barn owls and kestrels as they work their way up and down the lines of tussocks and wildflower, then disappear from view with a stoop to snaffle a furry lunch. The AB9 mix is ideally meant to last for three years, after which it will need swathing, cultivating and redrilling. The beetle banks, meanwhile, are more or less permanent, only being disturbed every seven years or so whenever mole draining is required. The Flea Barn's eastern beetle bank boasts a twenty-six-metre-wide block of AB8. It also contains a swathe of AB5 – the provision of habitat for nesting lapwing – which receives a grant of £566/ha/annum.

The lapwing is one of those birds we all took for granted in arable country. Much like the starling and the house sparrow, they seemed to disappear from our landscape almost overnight, without any notice. Their decline was in truth not sudden, but a steady downwards spiral which began post-Second World War, brought about, yet again, by the intensification of farming and to a marked degree by the expansion of greenfield building development. But by the mid-1980s, the shift from spring to autumn sowing, wholesale drainage and the absence of livestock all combined to create a nearly catastrophic decline in lapwing habitat and feeding sources. Their breeding productivity decelerated to an unsustainable level. The AB5 lapwing plot simulates the open fallow land that was once so commonplace and the birds require for nesting. This infield area, a minimum of one hectare in size, must be left bare of crop; if weeds cover more than 70 per cent of the plot, they must be sprayed off to retain the open-ground nature of this habitat. Many farmers across East Anglia embraced this seemingly simple conservation practice, despite the grant being less than generous. Over consecutive winters, the skies over Flea Barn saw lapwing flocks increase in size. We recorded these numbers in the annual Big Farmland Bird Count surveys run by the Game and Wildlife Conservation Trust (GWCT). In 2020 a blob of forty was noted, in 2021 sixty and, by February 2022, 124. The problem was, throughout this period, the lapwing had failed to read the script, as for that matter had the carrion crows. Despite all of the winter flocking activity overhead, only a single pair of lapwing ever chose to nest on the bespoke Flea Barn maternity unit. In 2020 we spied through binoculars the solitary pair laying their clutch of oversized khaki eggs on the open stubble. We watched and waited and hoped. At some point one morning, about a week into brooding, a carrion crow predated the nest. It is true we didn't see the act; the culprit could have been another corvid – a magpie or rook. We only found the shattered aftermath. But Gouldy knows corvid predation when he sees it – the eggshells lack the visible remnants of elastic membrane and the shards are bent inwards, all indicators that a powerful beak has accessed the yolky bounty within, rather than any chick struggling to get out. We'd lost our all-too-rare lapwings, predated by an all-too-common generalist predator. In late autumn 2021, Ed called time on the idea, deciding to cultivate the lapwing plot and sow a Bumble Bird mix in its place. This replacement combination of pollen, nectar, seed and cover would doubtless support his population of red-listed grey partridges instead, he figured. Ridiculously, the RPA could fine him for this pragmatic conservation-led decision.

The wonder of Flea Barn is not that this farm or its owner are extraordinary. It is more that this place is ordinary, and Ed is ordinary – 'just a farmer', as he describes himself. He is a humble man and shuns the limelight. I wrote a series of articles about our work at Flea Barn, determined to tell others about what he had achieved for wildlife by working smarter, using a combination of readily available grants and his knowledge as an expert grower. He allowed me to give tours of his farm to groups ranging from professional conservationists to members of the Young Farmers Club, to explain and expound the 'Flea Barn method' of hedges, edges, wetlands and woods. Ed's system unquestionably improved the biodiversity of the farm yet did no damage to his bottom line financially. I also noticed that the longer this conservation project went on, the more it became evident that Ed had fallen inextricably in love with the nature on his farm. He became as proud of his pairs of grey partridge, floristic margins and thick hedgerows filled with yellowhammer, goldfinches, linnet and buntings as he was of his yields of wheat, beans or oilseed rape. Nature improved his health.

I entered Flea Barn into the 2023 Purdey Awards. Ed received a Highly Commended from the judges. In other words, he came fourth, a remarkable achievement when one considers the sheer numbers of entrants in this prestigious conservation competition. We picked up our certificate in London, awash in champagne and our backs sore from slapping. Yet I was left with a niggling feeling that the judges had somewhat missed the point. At Flea Barn, Ed has created a replicable and repeatable template. This system of well-managed laid hedgerows abutting improved meadowland margins, with nodes of specialist habitat at the ends of each leafy, thorny 'river', is one that could be created and utilised on nearly every lowland arable farm. Ed continues to farm sustainably, yet equally he has secured a permanent home for wildlife. Flea Barn is a great example of why we mustn't think of the hedge as cure-all, or some sort of panacea. Hedges are a part of the puzzle, a very important one, but flower rich-margins, wetlands, food provision and predator control all equally matter too. Nature recovery has no simplistic answers; it is a sum of many complex parts. But the integral corner-piece in increasing biodiversity is the farmer. The truth is, if we are to see nature recover in England, we need more people like Ed. We need farmers who believe that ponds, insects, weeds, rough corners *and* hedges are not only beautiful, but integral to their businesses.

6

Bucolic

Grey murk and mist; the damp air soaks into the fibres of my woollen hat. My beard becomes heavy with water droplets, then they run down my neck. 'Rum old place,' I say to myself for the second time since I parked the truck alongside our hedge of the day. I unscrew the lid from my flask, pour myself a cup of sweet tea, then I raise my binoculars, twiddling my right index finger across the thumbwheel to focus them. Made by Steiner and encased in toughened rubber, the drab green optics live in the door pocket of my truck. I use them daily, and despite the constant abuse they get, they seem nearly indestructible. The watery flatness of the fenland landscape, the low cloud, reed, rinsed-out grasses and a tractor cultivating in the field beyond, pursued by gulls, all show in crystal clarity. There are yet more gulls wheeling overhead, and a skein of greylags; beneath them a line of trees and reeds in the dykes seem bent in prayer to the gloomy sky. As if painted by a watercolourist, Ely cathedral makes a fleeting appearance between clouds that glower over the seemingly endless horizon. 'How far away is that?' I ask the dogs. Mabel doesn't reply, nor does her daughter Blyth, who is now old enough to join us. Gouldy is late. I remember he has to drop off his daughter at school, and I feel alone under the great fenland sky. More tea, then I watch some more. I see long-tailed tits, chubby-cheeked with badger-pied faces. A tiny squadron of them goes rollercoasting out over the soaked grassland, making for the safety of the wood in synchronised bounds, excitedly cheeping in theatrical terror of imminent hooked-beak death.

Above the tits I see another bird, much larger. It veers sharp left in a flurry, looking for all the world like a discarded carrier bag set flapping by the wind. I twiddle the dial, there is mist on the lenses, and it comes into focus. The cock hen harrier flops and flaps in erratic flight. 'Sky dancer' some call them. I see his flat head swivel left and right, patrolling over reedy dykes, fully filled with dark water. His blue-grey plumage suits this blue-grey sky. In moments it is hard to tell where the heavens end and the harrier begins.

I put the caps back on the binoculars and replace them in my truck, then whistle the dogs from their snuffling to come for a fuss. As I straighten to stand, the lowering clouds part. A watery sun shines through for a moment, turning the cathedral gold in that instant, inspiring awe and wonder, even in someone as godless as me. Ancient and gothic, standing proud on its 'Isle of Eels', the building morphs to a gilded mountain, towering over this plain of flat, dark earth and reeds, tractors and water. The dogs undertake vigorous synchronised shaking. Both then jump willingly into the truck for a nap, black coats tousled and reeking. I remove my damp beanie and put on a chainsaw helmet. It feels chilled against my soaked head. I unwrap the old billhook from its swaddling of oily protective cloth and drag the lump hammer out from under an old feed sack. My boots squelch on grass and black soil as Gouldy draws up. Through his windscreen, I see he is on the phone as is normal; he daily endures multiple morning calls – poor sod is trying to buy a house and estate agents are the bane of his life. We have a little over 400 metres of hedge to lay and the cathedral spire has become lost amid the mist and murk. It will be a hard day in the thorny office.

An hour's drive west from my home, you leave the bulging border of Suffolk behind as you turn off the A14 and take the Newmarket road. Passing through Kennet then Kentford, you turn right at the Bell Inn, after which you are in Cambridgeshire: 'furrin' parts. The landscape changes slowly, the sky becomes bigger, the land starts to flatten. Then, with the suddenness of a flipped light switch, all is alien. Gone are the strong clays and gentle roll, the fields of cereals pockmarked with century-old pheasant coverts. Also gone, for the greater part, are the hedges. The monotonous flat fields, with soils coloured like black coffee, are edged instead by gaping ditches that can cope with a flood, or swallow my Isuzu truck in a watery gulp. Ditches are essential, wetly lining the mogul runs that pass for roads in this part of the country. So built up are these causeways, and so desiccated and shrunken is the land, that there is frequently a three- or four-metre fall from the metalled road to the agricultural land below. This moonscape of peat and dykes and thin belts of poplar windbreaks is the start of the Fens. The contrast between my gentle Suffolk, a mere hour away, with this stark Cambridgeshire makes them feel a million miles apart. The Fens are lonely and foreboding – to 'furriners' such as me they are, anyway. Lonely because this is a sparsely populated place; once off the main highway you are just as likely to meet a marsh harrier as a Hermes courier. The isolated farmhouses, sited seemingly at random, are invariably shielded from view by corrals of crack willow or poplar. It strikes me, as I drive along, that the properties I pass never feel like they nestle in these flat lands; they rise and stare at you, with more than a hint of menace. Meanwhile, housing in the villages crams itself into close-knit terraces, clinging to the higher, dryer ground. The 'feature properties' are Georgian. They look like rectories; they probably were until the church of England sold them off. The churches those vicars served are more ancient, mediaeval skyscrapers, but then anything here above sea level appears colossal. Farming in the Fens, however, shuns the ancient – it is cutting edge and takes centre stage, largely because the soil doesn't merely look like a growbag, it has all the vigorous fecundity of one too. I knew a professional rabbiter called Chris Earith who lived out west of Newmarket. He was a mine of fenland wisdom and could catch anything that crawled, ran or swam. 'You could throw a house brick into the middle of one of these fields and it would have a fair go at sprouting,' he told me. It is extraordinary stuff, 'fen peat over glaciofluvial drift'.

Big skies and black soils, tall tractors and barely a soul to be seen, the peat fen is a haunting place. There is a belief, admittedly one rarely carried by the locals, that this Cambridgeshire fenland was once nought but bog, reed and will-o'-the-wisp. That was until 1630, when the Duke of Bedford, along with his hired hand, Dutch engineer Cornelius Vermuyden, improved (or destroyed, depending upon your view) this place. Believe the stories, and before His Grace got busy, the whole region was almost devoid of man, stuffed with little else but wildfowl, waders, fish and wet miasma. This misty-eyed interpretation of history has helped lead to initial plans for 3,700 hectares of Cambridgeshire Grade 1 agricultural land, in between Huntingdon and Peterborough, to be rewetted (a moister version of rewilding). Called the Great Fen restoration, it is proposed to undo the work of Bedford and his Gentleman Adventurers, Vermuyden and his navvies. Whilst peat is the key to agricultural success here, it is simultaneously an Achilles heel to the UK's lofty ambitions for carbon net neutrality by 2050. Fourteen per cent of Britain's peat is found in the Cambridgeshire Fens, yet this area accounts for 56 per cent of our peat carbon emissions, largely due to the extensive drainage that enables intensive farming, the two of which combine to reduce the soil's carbon storage capabilities. The marketing materials published by a coalition of Wildlife Trusts and local authorities associated with the Great Fen show beautifully imagined, painted scenes of cranes flying over a waterlogged patchwork of rewetted Washes. Yet the more I searched for the government's drivers for the project (both Natural England and the Environment Agency are co-partners in the Great Fen), the more it appeared their interest has little to do with lost flora and fauna and a whole lot to do with carbon. The truth seems to be that the farmers and people of the Fens are having to make way for water not so much so that nature can recover, but in order for the government to meet the carbon emission and sequestration guarantees it made at COP26. A question nagged me as I sat on my truck tailgate, watching harriers and waiting for Gouldy to arrive and start laying that hedge: is rewilding this place, is creating a 'Great Fen' (and a slated expansion of the project to rewet 75 per cent more of this most fertile agricultural region) truly a good thing for the environment, the wildlife and the people of the Fens, or not?

Francis Pryor, one of our most distinguished living archaeologists, and a Fen Tiger himself to his grubby fingertips, has spent a lifetime excavating in both the peat-lands of the south-western Fens and the silt Fens further north, next the Wash. His book *The Fens* is about his lifetime spent digging up the past in the peat. It is fascinating. It catalogues the tantalising marks of East Anglia's history. We learn this is largely an agricultural history, dating back thousands of years before Vermuyden started draining. Most tantalising is his recollection of a dig at Fengate near Peterborough. Pryor, along with a team from Cambridge, began excavating a thigh-deep, man-made ditch. This shallow dyke was clearly dug to drain water rather than act as a barrier to man or livestock. There they unearthed, within a waterlogged pit, a 'thick twig, grown in a characteristically jerky fashion with right-angled bends'. Pryor, a sheep farmer in his spare time, understands the true significance of this blackthorn barb, shaped like a capital 'L'. Radiocarbon dating proved the 'jerky twig', perfectly preserved in the peat, was a piece of 4,000-year-old hedgelayer's brash – right-angled growth such as this only occurs as a result of man cutting blackthorn. I like to think the blade that made that cut was a billhook, highly prized no doubt and crafted from bronze. If hedgelayers were at large in 2000 BC fenland, it stands to reason that hedges had long been planted here, certainly sufficiently advanced in growth to require management prescriptions little different from those Gouldy and I use today. Further excavations at Fengate uncovered sheep droves and what appeared to be a livestock market. This unearthing of managed hedges, well-dug drainage ditches, and sheep farming at a proto-commercial scale, indicates that arable would inevitably have been a feature here too. After all, sheep need sustenance in winter and man cannot live solely on mutton, trapped fish and wildfowl. Agriculture, in all its forms, was therefore demonstrably a significant feature of the Fens, long before Vermuyden got digging. Pryor had discovered the earliest evidence of a managed hedge anywhere in Europe, and where there are hedges there is farming.

The Fens, then, have for over 4,000 years been a place where farming has thrived and evolved. Nature has had 400 centuries of adapting, evolving and learning to rub along with humans and our agricultural practices. Essentially, humans made the Fens and we belong here, I believe, just as much as the teal, the harrier, or the eel. Francis Pryor's excavations in the Fens are fascinating. He has no monolithic stones or barrows and tumuli to guide his spade. This land has few stones, and the peat is far too sodden to allow tombs to be dug deep. He relies solely upon his understanding of the soil and the subtle tales it tells. It is only thanks to his remarkable knowledge of the peat that we now know the truth of the Fens. Man has, for at least 4,500 years, dug, drained and delved, grown crops and reared livestock here. Fenland was farmland and continues to be farmland. All that has changed is the scale and intensity.

Clearly, the draining of the Fens in the 1630s boosted the capability of the locals to farm more efficiently. Ongoing drainage, new cuts and pumping systems powered by wind, then steam, then electricity, brought new land into cultivation. The peat soil found beneath these former wetlands is remarkably fertile and notably fragile. Those raised causeways along which I drive are only at their giddy heights because the peat soil, once exposed, becomes oxidised. Denuded of moisture it begins to shrink like a drying sponge and grains blow away in the wind. Although the Fens comprise a mere 4 per cent of England's total land mass, this region produces one third of our fresh food. The sheer luxury of this super-soil's dark richness means this is the very best place to grow vegetables and salad crops, cut flowers and bulbs – rich returns from rich soil. The 80,000 people estimated to be employed by the fenland food chain rely on that peat; the exchequer, too, is partial to its cut of the £3 billion per annum generated by all of that food production. It is more than curious, then, that the government is even contemplating relinquishing so much of this profitable, fertile and economically vital chunk of England, and flooding it in order to create a carbon sink.

The hedge where I watched the sky dancer hunt was one of five we had to lay at Hainey Farm. This particular hedge Gouldy and I 'conservation laid' – a process that has no notion of stock proofing, beauty or traditionalism. Using a style we developed that concentrates on thickening up the hedge from the base, side branches are only removed on the 'downhill side'; the sides and top are left bushy. Conservation laying shuns the rigid prescriptions of the thirty recognised regional hedgelaying styles developed for stock proofing. Instead, this conservation style, although carried out with close attention to building a robust and sturdy hedge, is done solely for the benefit of wildlife. We have evolved and adapted an existing system advocated by Richard Adams, a professional West Country hedger. Where Richard laid his pleachers without any stakes, we pollard an upright limb every one-and-a-half metres or so. We lay the next few pleachers into these 'living stakes', as we call them, repeating the process along the whole length. 'Crooking' – or securing – the hedge in this way is essential in the exposed large-field landscapes of the east, where winds blow straight from Siberia. Pollarding 'living stakes' also removes the need for time-consuming hazel coppicing. Conservation laying may be markedly less aesthetic than the hedges where we employ traditional staked and bound techniques, yet for all that, the farmland birds that live within, the mammals in the understorey, the insects that feed and breed and lay their eggs on the leaves and branches don't care one fig. Wildlife has no time for the look of things – scenery and tradition are human passions. All wildlife wants is sex, food, protection and habitat – conservation laying lacks the bucolic, but on the right sort of hedge, in the right sort of place, it provides three of those things; we leave the sex to nature. I believe that this form of hedgelaying was most likely the earliest 'style' ever employed. The idea that a hedger would carry armfuls of stakes and binders with him to a job, when his only means of transport was his own two legs, is implausible. It amuses me greatly how the general public so adores the straight lines and clinical precision of a championship-winning hedge, yet the linnets are utterly indifferent.

Hainey Farm sits in the middle of low-lying peat fen in between picturesquely ecclesiastical Ely, the 'Isle of Eels', and the less picturesque small town of Soham, a conurbation with a name that has evolved from the Anglo-Saxon *Soegham*, meaning soggy. 'Eels and sogginess' – a fenland epithet if ever there was one. The Shropshire family owns Hainey Farm; it is organic and one small part of their enterprise – G's Fresh Farm

Produce. The Shropshires are a fine example of the entrepreneurial, somewhat dogged, spirit of fenlanders. In 1952 Guy Shropshire (the G in G's) bought 330 acres near Ely where he grew earth-covered celery, which he harvested and packed into traditional bushel boxes. These he sold on to wholesalers. He soon realised he could increase his returns if he cut out the middleman and invested in his own vegetable-washing and -packing plant. By 1960 his celery, all washed and packed in-house, left the farm and went directly to retailers. Fast forward to today, and G's own, and farm, 20,000 hectares of fenland, along with holdings in Eastern Europe, Spain and Senegal, supplying year-round veg, salad and root crops to retailers. From a starting point of a few hundred acres in the 1950s, the enterprise is now one of Europe's largest fresh food producers. This family farm is a salutary reminder that agriculture is a business, no different from any other business. Fail to innovate, fail to remain relevant, fail to modernise and the business fails. G's is also an example of the curious relationship that the British public, and our media, have with farming and farmers. British companies outside agriculture who thrive and expand, becoming large-scale employers and income generators, are celebrated, held up as paragons of Blighty's entrepreneurial spirit and canny ways. With farming, however, enterprises such as G's are derided, sneeringly called 'agri-business' as if this is a title of shame, an example of excess and greed. It is odd indeed that someone like Lord Sainsbury is perceived as the good guy, yet a Mr Shropshire is the baddy.

Each generation of Shropshires has focused and refocused its attention on agricultural innovation and improvement, reflecting market needs, sometimes leading the market itself. Guy clearly understood that fresh-food preparation and packaging were factors that mattered to both the consumer and the retailer; his restructuring of these areas kept the end user loyal and boosted his own bottom line. By increasing profits, the farm was able to expand; agriculture is invariably more successful when at scale. Guy's sons, John and Peter, when they joined the business, looked at the science of production. They asked how best the land could be worked, what varieties could be grown profitably, and they thought hard about what consumers and supermarkets wanted. Then came the grandsons. Guy Shropshire Jnr consolidated the business, modernising machinery and increasing their productive landholdings. His younger brother, Charles, innovated in a different way, or, as he says, 'future-proofed the farm and a large part of the Fens'. Charles's forebears had worked out what to grow, how to grow it, package it and present it in the most profitable manner. Charles focused his attention on the land itself, understanding that he and his family owed this soil everything. To repay this debt, he looked at new ways of farming in a world that was more cost-conscious yet simultaneously demanded the highest environmental standards of production – all the time, of course, with the supermarkets' hand gripped tight to his throat. As a passionate conservationist, Charles sought to balance running a profitable business with nature recovery. Allied to this, thanks to government diktat, G's had to become a carbon storage and sequestration facilitator. Whitehall had promised the world that Britain would be the greenest of green countries. To achieve this our government expected the farmers of Britain to carry the can in honouring the promises they had made. Charles is on the road to doing that, with the help of a man called Stew.

Stewart Macintyre is a gamekeeper. He looks like a professional rugby player, twinkly-eyed and six foot five. The permanent Desperate Dan stubble on his square jaw suits him. I have an inkling he would be a handy man to have alongside you if a pub argument turned into a brawl. At Hainey Farm, they do things a bit bigger and better than most. Therefore Stewart is not solely a gamekeeper; he is the manager of G's game and wildlife division. His team comprises an underkeeper and three dedicated machinery operators. Along with the more standard keepering tasks of rearing pheasants and partridges, controlling predators and agricultural pests, and managing supplementary feeding, he is the man given responsibility for actioning Charles Shropshire's remarkable vision for nature recovery. His work also benefits the farm. Stew guarantees the environmental provenance of the food that is grown here. The retailers that sell G's organic crops are forward thinking; they have savvy customers who care not only about taste and quality, but also want a guarantee that their food has been grown with forethought and environmental consideration. Admittedly these shoppers are sufficiently wealthy to make environment-friendly choices; the supermarkets where they shop charge premium prices, certainly when compared to those selling imported fayre from countries where exacting standards of food production are looser or just plain ignored.

In the spring prior to our commencing laying the Hainey hedges, I toured the farm with Stewart and Charles. We paused in a newly planted copse of silver birch and thorn, where I asked Charles about the government's plans to rewet the Fens. He waved his hand towards the farmland that lay before us, a patchwork of veg, cover crops and citrus-green well-tillered wheat. In the distance, a wall of nearly indentical houses marking a recently erected housing estate on Soham's edge stared stark. 'All that,' Charles said, 'would be flooded,' adding with a pained grin, 'unless, that is, I keep my pumps running. It's not very wild, really, is it?' I thought of the 10,000 people who live in Soham and wondered how they felt about becoming 'soggy'. 'Can they do that? Flood your land whether you like it or not?' I asked, 'They think they can,' Charles replied. He changed the subject in a trice. 'I want to show you what Stew has been up to,' and scurried back to his vehicle. Charles is a man forever on the go, constantly moving. When he talks his facial expressions reveal his mind is already on another topic; busy man, busy grimy hands black with peat, he reminds me of one of my spaniels. He is never still.

Stew stood waiting for me with his hands on his hips atop an earthen bank. The subsoil bund of clay was still marked by the tracks of heavy diggers that had created this wetland. I joined him and looked down on acres of water, inlets and reed. Blue-clay islands thrust up through the ripple like rolling trout, already becoming carpeted with grasses, sedges and reed. A pair of startled moorhens spluttered off, paddling furiously towards the margins. Teal sprang away in a pack of six; these dainty ducks are remarkably shy. Greylags dabbled, grumbling a dog-like growl from their carrot beaks to let us know that we were not welcome here. Out in deeper water, mallard patrolled, necks hunched into their bodies, looking for all the world like toy boats. Black-headed gulls bobbed too, these dandies seeming nonplussed by man, knowing that tall Stew is something of an ally. After all, he fills the feeders that ring this haven of water, reed and wonder. A marsh tit clung to a reed-mace stem, the soft breeze causing his perch to wave like a banner. Dowdy dunnocks bounced about in and under the scrubby hawthorn, seething and squeaking, wary but not so scared to believe an immediate exit was necessary. 'What do you think?' Stew asked. 'Amazing,' I replied, and I really meant it.

I swiftly gleaned that at Hainey they have used their field corners and less productive areas in much the same manner as Ed has done at Flea Barn when creating floristic meadows and scrub. Yet this is the Fens, a one-time land of water, drained, and now, in parts, being returned to water. Charles and Stew have reintroduced wetlands and ponds and meres across the farm, not in the arbitrary wholesale way that rewetting would have had it, but in a managed way, a conservationist's way. The bund on which we both stood was high enough to retain the water, while on the far bank gulleys are carved out, acting as overflows, running into larger drainage channels. These channels and dykes are controlled by pumps; indeed, this whole landscape only exists thanks to pumps and drains. The Fens in their way are like hedgerows. Both are man-made, yet neither can be truly tamed. Without regular tweaks and additions – a digger-bucket of clay here, a channel dug there, a switch of a pump – and all of this land goes back under water, just as a hedge becomes a monoculture line of straggly trees without the intervention of chainsaw and billhook. I listened to Stew and discovered that a practical conservationist's role here is as much about being a civil engineer as it is about a life spent feeding and trapping, enhancing and planting. Stew explained how under all of that rippling wet, a well-planned sculptured topography lies. Shallows and sand bars are created, the islands are moulded from blue clay in the manner in which my wife, a potter, throws a lump onto her wheel. This is all just as planned, micro-managed and just as important to the wildlife as any of Stew's feeders or blocks of wild-bird seed, or even his hedges. The depths and the shallows reflect the requirements of countless different species – think of the man-made RSPB Minsmere, a place regarded as a 'conservation jewel in Suffolk's crown'. It is the same here at Hainey. The only difference being that this is paid for by a canny farmer's profits, not the efforts of canny fundraisers and generous donors.

These manufactured wetlands maximise every centimetre of their mass. After all, one cannot be profligate; Grade 1 agricultural land such as this is precious and valuable. Hundreds of thousands of tons of organic lettuce, onions, celery, beetroot and pak choi that we all relish eating are grown here, alongside these human-dug lakes and human-planted woods, hedges, strips and seed blocks. The Shropshire model for creating plentiful space for wildlife is not done via the clumsiness of blocking up the drains and rewetting great swathes, because it makes neither financial sense nor any natural sense. Nor does rewetting the Fens return it to any 'original' state: as we have seen, the Fens have, since 4000 BC, been farmland. The Shropshires also understand that, on a human level, rewetting is a non-starter too. The people of Soham and countless other fenland towns and villages, the people who sow, grow and pick the crops, or pack them, or drive the lorries carrying tray after tray of fresh produce: none have any wish to be soggy. It would take only one failed pump to cause a wide-scale inundation. Much of Soham is over two metres below the water table, as a report by the town's council into further housing developments revealed; a breach of the river Great Ouse at Soham Lode would result in catastrophic flooding. The fact that Stew has created this home for wildlife, rather than leaving it up to nature via 'rewilding', matters not one jot to the wildlife. After all, nature doesn't *eat* scenery. Far better for them that they have multiple rough corners, sown blocks, planted copses, managed belts, created marshes, dug ponds and laid hedges, far better for us that we can still eat the bounty that this farm produces. Of course, all these wonders of copse and scrub and wetness need linking together to make a whole. This is largely achieved at Hainey Farm by the hedge, which of course is why I was there at all.

Stew's activation of Charles's plans leans heavily on hedgerows because the hedge is the great connector. Connectivity is an integral factor in this conservation model. The lee of the hedge is where supplementary food is provided by Stew on his quad bike with a spinner attached to the back. His pheasants and partridges tuck in, and so do the yellowhammers and linnets, goldfinches, hedge sparrows and reed buntings. The traps that he sets to catch stoats and rats he places within the hedge in human-made tunnels; the Larsen traps that catch the corvids are sited alongside the hedge. All of this predator control means all the more lapwings and plovers, more grey partridges, more tits, warblers and passerines – all of the birds of the Fens. His integral wetland features would be mere island habitats without this connectivity provided by hedges. The hedgerows also connect his new copses. Native saplings of silver birch and white willow, holm oak and London plane – all species that grow well in the Fens – have been planted and guarded. These trees have been undersown with wildflowers that will thrive in the short term; once the trees mature, the shade they cast over the meadowland flora will lead many to decline; they will have done their job for pollinators for the time being. But this is a managed place. The trees, once mature, will be thinned and the hazel coppiced for use as hedging binders and stakes. Sunlight will once more reach the understorey; woodland flower species, their seed blown in by the wind or borne in by bird shit, will erupt; a human-made copse morphs into a naturalised wood in a remarkably short time. This glory of course will not all come to fruition until Charles and Stew are themselves long under the peat soil, but theirs is forward-thinking conservation. They do things today that have positive effects in the future as well as today.

Some of the scrub species that Stew and his team plant are not natives at all. Among the hawthorns and blackthorns, dog rose and guelder, I spied clumps of thuja, Christmas trees and laurel. 'The traditionalists won't like these,' I say to Stew, plucking my thumb and forefinger on the waxy glabrous leaf of a cherry laurel. 'Fuck 'em,' he replies with a laugh. 'The birds need the shelter now.' He is correct, of course. The laurels, lonicera and firs may not be native, but they provide enormous benefits in short order. This is the conundrum of conservation. Some rewilding advocates deride Stew's digging and planting and sowing as 'gardening'. Rewilding works on the principle that nature, given time, will heal itself, which is probably true. But Stew believes the fenland wildlife doesn't have the luxury of time. He says it requires his help right now, in what could be described as its darkest hour. It is a mindset that suits Hainey Farm and suits the Fens. This land has been altered and moulded by man for so many years, as that 4,000-year-old piece of blackthorn so clearly shows. 'How,' Stew asks, 'do you rewild this place? It has never known what wild is.'

At Hainey, every piece of land that can be farmed productively, sustainably and efficiently, is. Land that cannot be is still farmed just as intensively, but now the 'crop' is wildlife. It is true that the aesthetics of this method of conservation-led land management is much like our conservation-style laid hedges. The network of seed blocks, woods, wetlands and hedgerows is notably less bucolic to the human eye, certainly when compared to the scenes portrayed by the artist's impression of the 'Great Fen', but it begs the question: does bucolic matter to wildlife? The RSPB and BTO helped Charles record the bird and mammal life at Hainey Farm. These were added to Stew's own extensive records. They give clear and irrefutable evidence that the creation and human management of habitat, the provision of food, and targeted predator control creates not only positive results for nature, but also dovetails with sustainable and profitable arable and vegetable production. Could Charles give over these hundreds of acres to wildlife if he didn't farm the land? Could or should he rewild and rewet these thousands of hectares? He believes the straight answer is 'no'. It is only thanks to the profitability of his farming practices that he can afford, admittedly with the support of Defra stewardship grants, to employ Stew and his team. If he rewilded the farm in the style of Knepp, he could be bankrupt in a decade. Could he rely on people wanting to camp in a field two feet below the water table?

Another question is even more important. What would happen to this farm and its wildlife if Charles gave up, sold up and put the land on the market as a rewilding project? A billionaire could buy the place and fund a 20,000-hectare project, a Great, Great Fen if you will. But what about the human cost? This is the place where our organic veg is grown, and a hectare yields twelve tonnes of wheat. This is the place where thousands of people work. This is the place where tens of thousands of people live. This is the place that feeds millions of us. Does that mean that projects like the Great Fen should be scrapped? It is doubtless true that rewilding or rewetting is a wonderful notion. In theory rewilding the Fens is superb for wildlife (although this is a wholly theoretical model in the UK, devoid of any landscape-scale practical research). It is probable that rewetting the Fens could lead to the restoration of threatened species. The question is, are words such as 'probable' and 'could' enough to take such a leap? If you visit Hainey Farm when they open the farm gate on Open Farm Sunday each June, and meet Charles and his team, if you watch the wildlife that surrounds you in this 'rum old place', you swiftly learn it is not the end of farming in the Fens that will make nature recovery a reality. It is farming better, farming smarter, farming like a Shropshire that will do so.

Farming in the Fens does have an environmental Achilles heel. The act of tilling peat soils actively releases carbon into the atmosphere. Studies conducted by Fenland SOIL* revealed that 40 per cent of Cambridgeshire's carbon emissions come from agricultural land use in the Fens. In a bid to counter this fact, the government told fenland farmers that 75 per cent of lowland peat areas must be rewetted by 2050. It is not fully understood where this precise figure of 75 per cent came from, but the solution for locking away the required tonnes of carbon through raising the water tables, thereby effectively ending traditional farming in the Fens, came from scientists based at the Centre for Ecology and Hydrology and the University of Leicester. This is not to denigrate their solution. The academics were asked the somewhat singular question, 'How do we reduce agricultural CO_2 emissions in the Fens by 75 per cent?' and they answered it. They weren't called upon to include in their conclusions how to protect people's livelihoods and homes,

---

* Fenland SOIL is a not-for-profit organisation that brings farmers, academics, conservationists and the local population together to find a holistic solution to the challenges of food, farming and the environment in the Fens.

support nature recovery, and ensure food continues to get onto people's plates.

I returned to Hainey Farm in May to check on the regrowth of the hedges Gouldy and I had conservation-laid the previous December. I organised a meeting there with Megan Hudson, the general manager of Fenland SOIL. Megan is a local farmer's daughter, therefore no stranger to this idiosyncratic landscape. I asked her about the efficacy of the proposed flooding of the Fen peat-lands to capture and retain carbon. It is, she says, not without its problems. I discovered that if peat is flooded to a depth of over thirty centimetres, while the carbon is certainly locked up, methane and nitrous dioxide are released. These two latter greenhouse gases are widely acknowledged to be an equal if not greater contributor to global warming than carbon. This comes as no groundbreaking news to the local 'Fen Tigers'. Their moniker was coined to reflect not so much any ferocious temperament (admittedly a night out in Soham can get rowdy at closing time) as the roaring asthmatic sound the old peat cutters made, having breathed in a noxious cocktail of gases for years as they dug out spade after spade of the wet peat to then dry for fuel. The more I listened to Megan, the more I realised that if the stop boards were put in the dykes, the drains were blocked and the pumps turned off – if this landscape saw farming cease and become rewetted as advocated by a number of the leading NGOs and backed by local and national government – the outcome would be, at best, questionable for fenland wildlife. For the people here it would be disastrous, with little to no environmental positives. If flooded, the higher areas of the Fens would dry out, continuously emitting CO_2. The lower zones would become too wet and emit CH_4 and NO_2. Some parts might be just right, but these would still require constant management by pumps and drainage. If we lost Hainey Farm and the other fecund farms hereabouts, we would face a 25 per cent downturn in our fresh-food production, forcing us to import vegetables and salads from countries where environmental considerations in farming are an afterthought. We would need to find jobs for 80,000 people made redundant from the fenland food production industry. The longer I listened, the more I shook my head in disbelief. How had the idea of rewetting the Fens made it off the back of a fag packet?

For all that, greenhouse-gas emissions are a genuine concern in farming. In Suffolk's clay soils, carbon can be locked away via minimising soil disturbance – that is, using a direct drill rather than traditional ploughing. Carbon can also be 'fixed' by sowing leguminous or brassica cover crops. These are companion-drilled under wheat, barley, oilseed rape etc., and is becoming common practice in 'regen farming' models. Unfortunately, peat soils behave in a different way from clay. Dotted across Hainey Farm's peat sit strange-looking pieces of electronic gadgetry, called flux towers. These hugely expensive devices carry sensors which measure the exchanges of carbon dioxide, water vapour and energy between the peat and the atmosphere. The towers indicate when carbon is being released, invariably during cultivating, drilling or harvesting. With the carbon emission levels across the farm now a known quantity thanks to these towers, the Hainey team are experimenting with methods of mitigation. Working alongside agri-scientists from parts of Europe and Canada with soils similar to those found in the Fens, G's and fourteen other fenland farmers are exploring ways to achieve carbon-friendly agriculture. They have looked at trials in Germany and Holland that used 'wet crops' – reeds and sedges, which thrive in a flooded environment; fibres sourced from these perennial plants can be used in the manufacture of fabrics or building materials, or as biofuel. They are of course inedible, so fail to provide any food security. Other trials include adding carbon-stabilising materials to the peat, including wood-chip and biochar. More straightforward yet was the realisation that if rewetting the Fens stored carbon, so too could irrigation, as already happens in crop production. The flux towers reveal that carbon emissions from the soil are dramatically reduced during periods when growing crops are watered. The notion of continuing the irrigation process twelve months of the year, particularly whenever dry periods occur, is not only an eminently practical way of ensuring carbon storage, but also potentially future-proofs the Fens for both humans and wildlife. Megan spoke to me about 'inverted hedges': ditches that maintain the drainage of the land and carry the water used in irrigation. These ditches, too, can be managed for wildlife, their banks sown with reed and scrub, a margin introduced alongside them to create nesting habitats and drying grounds, providing habitat connectivity just like my 'proper' hedges. 'You can't lay an inverted hedge, can you?' I joked to Megan. She looked at me with tired eyes. She had just spent a week at a conference trying to promote the Hainey model of fenland conservation to men in suits. Poor humour was the last thing she needed.

'This place is and always has been farmland,' Megan said as we made our goodbyes. 'It's our job to make sure that this place continues to be farmland, and to work for nature and the environment.' I thought about her words as I checked the regrowth on our conservation-laid hedge. The hen harriers were absent. It was May and they'd long since left the Fens, making their way north to nest among the heather of the upland peat bogs. I also thought of Francis Pryor as I picked a piece of thorn brash from the cleat of my boot. I wondered what the hedgelayer of 4,000 years ago would have felt about the floods and flux towers and carbon storage. Much the same as me, most likely – a bit befuddled. I crouched down to look at the zesty shoots of hawthorn erupting from a cut stool and took a picture with my mobile phone to send to Gouldy. I watched a pair of long-tailed tits flit in the fronds, busy with their nest-making duties. One clutched a clump of moss in its beak, the other a duck breast-feather that curled over its pied face like an Ascot hat. Rum old place, the Fens.

Deadly Darren

Out on the marsh it is never truly dark. The moon may be long gone, but the stars remain, as does Venus, juddering away like the headlamp of a motorbike lurching its way over the potholes of a Suffolk B road. Sunrise is two hours away, yet the eastern horizon has a sodium glare; lights from the engineering plant, where they fabricate wind turbines, bring a false dawn. Peering through the foreground fringe of reeds and on far across the marsh, I can see a flickering UV flare as a welder works on some monstrous tower or snow-white blade. In time these mighty constructions will be out at sea, their bases battered by the brutish swell, their sails rotating, churning out clean energy and chopping migrating woodcock to pieces. The east coast has forever been a place of sails and wind, pumping water and grinding grain.

The stars and the planets may be mere flickering wicks yet when en masse, as they are this morning, they provide sufficient milky candlepower for me to see my flask and Darren seated alongside me. An insomniac redshank blows his usual tune, *pew, pew, pew*. The call tails off with half-hearted intonation, as if the wader had lost his train of thought. The redshanks seem to delight in beating the curlew to the punch in the 'who shouts first contest' of the salty dawn: of the calls of all the waders, warblers, finches, hawks, falcons, wildfowl and gulls that live in these marshes, I think I like the redshank's the best.

'Wigeon,' Darren whispers, and my eyes follow his upstretched arm, a black sleeve against the nearly-black and the stars. A shiver of whispering wings passes over where we hide in the mud and ooze and reed. *Eeoo* the pack, some fifty or so strong, whistle as they cross. The near light plays tricks, the little chocolate ducks seem unnaturally swift, scudding their way to Breydon Water, where they will feed and sleep and bob in the churning confluence of the triplet rivers Yare, Waveney and Bure. Darren and I crane our necks skyward, then stare left and right, quiet conversation punctuated at points by my stifled laughter and his filthy jokes.

Over the sea wall and across the shimmering tidal river, hidden from our view, a babble begins at the cue of true dawn in the east. The merest smear of purple, bringing with it an imperceptible breath of warmth . . . this is all it takes to wake them. First a pair, then a dozen begin their chatter – clear and perfect in the Norfolk November air comes the sound of conversations from the reeds on the far bank. Dozens more join in. Within minutes, one thousand pink-footed geese are squabbling and talking and planning their day. A thousand more and then another thousand, the rapture rises, an audio counterpoint to the visual splendour of this new morning. Pinks are cavalry trumpeters, sounding reveille for this part of the coast, the first place in Britain to see the sun each day. I now have to shout at Darren to be heard over the *wink, wink, wink*.

The geese are airborne, and skein after skein choose this precise moment to rise up from their roosts along this grim, glorious marshland. They smudge their way across the firmament, where the west is still night and the east is now day. We hunker down in our hide, gloved hands gripping the fore-ends of our guns; we are birdwatchers no more and hunters we become. Shielding our moon faces with camouflage masks, we pull hats down low on our brows. The decoys we set out in the dark two hours earlier now look a pale pastiche compared with the living wonder of the geese on the wing overhead. Straggling lines yelp like packs of hounds as they string out in their shrieking joyous Vs, making the staring, wheeling gulls seem pathetic and the mallard miniscule. Nature at this moment is nothing but geese and more geese. The sun, in the minutes that we were fixated by geese, has slunk fully over the horizon, bringing with it a cloud bank in off the sea. The sky palate through which the geese fly is manic, lines of orange, then tangerine under purple, leaving a topknot of deepest blue and silver; Venus still twinkles. *Wink, wink* behind us. Pinks, like the dawn sun, creep up on you. Darren whispers for the sake of whispering. On whiffling wings the first crosses of pinks pass over the reeds behind which we hide. *Wink, wink*. Darren puffs his cheeks on a wooden call and *wink, wink*s back in perfect imitation. Our knees shuffle in the reeking mud of the gutter, heads still down. 'Now,' Darren says, and we rise up like wraiths, guns to our shoulders. Shots ring, ears ring and geese fall, spiralling down to splash in unpoetic, unmagnificent death on the sodden sward. *Wink, wink*, the skein continues, the sound dwindling as they wing away to the fields inland, oblivious that three of their number lie dead behind them. It is never truly quiet, out here on the marsh. When the geese have passed, a flute from a curlew and a water rail's pig-like grunt fill the sound-void. Our dogs get busy retrieving the birds. The sky is bright, the stars gone, Venus forgotten. The rest of the human world will be waking soon, and we pack away our decoys and nets, then trudge the mile off the marsh.

THE NOTION THAT A conservationist, a self-proclaimed bird lover, a 'champion' of nature (as I was embarrassingly introduced to the guests before giving an after-dinner speech at the Hadleigh Agricultural Association's annual booze-up) can take some level of enjoyment from shooting a bird is, to some, totally incongruous. It remains, if I am honest, slightly incongruous to me too, and I have been shooting for over forty years now. The hunter's paradox – the idea of conserving, protecting, even loving a bird or animal while simultaneously setting out to kill that bird or animal – is a subject flogged to death by philosophers, writers, and angry people on social media. Wildfowling – the pursuit of ducks, geese and some wader species in and around coastal areas – exemplifies the paradox. To be a wildfowler, or at least to be any good as a wildfowler, first you must become an apprentice, intimately immersing yourself in a watery, stinking, lonely landscape. Wildfowling is no mere sea-wall ramble. You put yourself in places your parents told you not to go when you were young. Below the high-water mark of the foreshore, or on marshes filled with dangers, wading through estuarine mud or clinging to a grassy islet, which in flood may or may not become ten foot under. Fail to understand and respect the tides and winds and currents of these coastal wilds and you end up dead. Once you have studied and explored and have become a part of the marsh, then you must turn ornithologist.

Fowling is not a free-for-all. Before you become a full member of my club, the Great Yarmouth Wildfowlers, you must first endure a year's probation spent under the watchful eye of an experienced fowler. Assessment is ongoing, ensuring that you are safe, and that you can identify which birds you may shoot and which you may not. The duck species that can legally be shot are mallard, wigeon, teal, pintail, shoveler, gadwall, tufted, pochard and goldeneye. Goose shooting is restricted to greylag, pinkfoot, white-front, Egyptian and Canada. Snipe, woodcock and golden plover are the waders that can be shot. Shoot what you shouldn't and at best you could receive a fine and a jail sentence, at worst you incur the wrath of people like Darren and every other salty fowler in the East. If you mistake a cormorant on the horizon for a goose, it'll be spoken about for years; you'll be forever derided as a buffoon, a person you would never want to share a muddy ditch with.

While avid coastal birdwatchers nestle in purpose-built hides in purpose-built reserves, the fowler must go feral and venture far away from his fellow humans, to go where the wildfowl live. You can only hunt a duck or a goose if you first recognise their ways and their wiles, and after all of that, only then might you place yourself under their flightpath, very occasionally. The fieldcraft required to secrete yourself from these watchful birds is worthy of a sniper. Add to this the need to be within forty yards of your duck if you want to kill it, and you understand why it is that most ventures to the foreshore result in an empty gamebag and a cartridge belt as full as when you arrived. Therefore, to love these wild lands and waters, to adore the wildfowl, indeed all of the birds of the coast, is a prequisite. No one whose driver is ritualised slaughter or bloodlust would habitually rise at 3 a.m., don eight layers of clothing, drive to the coast, wade through mud, eat mud, wallow in mud accompanied by a muddy dog and a muddy gun, with muddy decoys, in sleet and rain, to invariably not shoot a single thing.

In the eight seasons since I first embarked upon this frankly lunatic activity, my friend Darren Sizer has taught me all of the little I know about wildfowling. He is, I would say, my best friend, which, I admit, sounds a somewhat childish thing for a fifty-four-year-old man to claim. Darren is single-minded, steadfastly refuses to suffer fools, and is an obsessive about the natural world. I have shivered in arm-flapping misery atop Aldeburgh's sea wall, waiting for him to finish marvelling at feeding snow buntings fresh in from Greenland. He knows a whimbrel from a curlew at a distance of a mile. He showed me how to squeak like a mouse on the back of your hand so that a hunting barn owl comes to investigate, cautioning, 'Mind, never try this with short-eared owls,' removing his woolly hat to reveal talon marks still scored across his balding pate. I once stood alongside him on the Breydon sea wall to watch the spectacle of 10,000 migrating wigeon on the wing. I swear he cried. I also once saw Darren throw into a dyke a man whom he caught being cruel to a dog. Yet for all that I give him the prefix 'Deadly Darren' in my *Shooting Times* articles, reflecting his accurate marksmanship and the seeming dispassionate ease with which he shoots a left and right of geese up on high. He is as Suffolk as Adnams (admittedly he doesn't drink alcohol) and the embodiment of the hunter's paradox. Darren the naturalist, Darren the hunter, Darren the game farmer.

Game shooting was once not so different from wildfowling. The late-Regency sportsman would heft his Damascus-barrelled muzzle-loader, pop his powder monkey, shot and caps in his bag, unkennel a pointer or field spaniel, and then sally forth to 'walk up' his quarry. There were no certainties he'd fill his game bag because the game he hunted was wild and wily. However, grey partridge were abundant in the eighteenth and nineteenth centuries, before the industrialisation of lowland farmland. The pheasant, too, was common. Although a native of Asia, pheasants have certainly been UK residents since the tail-end of the Roman occupation. The Normans also brought pheasants with them over the Channel, along with rabbits, fallow deer and hares. By the sixteenth century the pheasant was an English commoner and by the period our Regency gunner was active, they had long adapted to our temperate climate and landscape of food-rich, well-hedged and wooded farmland. Our sportsman would not have seen many red-legged partridge on his ramblings. These diminutively attractive gamebirds, natives of Spain, Portugal and southern France, are relative newcomers. Following failed attempts at their introduction in the seventeenth century, at some time around 1770 the Marquis of Hertford tried and succeeded in hatching, rearing and releasing several thousand he imported from France. From those initial introductions, the red-legged partridge slowly gained a foothold, and by the 1930s was well established across the milder half of England.

Game shooting, much like farming, slowly morphed into its current form thanks to innovation and advances in technology. By the mid-nineteenth century, the muzzle-loaders with their fiddly percussion caps and primers and ram rods were old hat, superseded by breech-loading double-barrelled guns. Nitro replaced black powder, providing more power, less smoke, more range. Sportsmen could now shoot faster and shoot more

The technological advances in shotguns played a significant part in changing the way the English landscape looked. Landowners planted woods with pheasant shooting in mind. The edges were planted up with shrub species, then laid to act as windbreaks; rides were cut so that light would filter down, sunning the backs of the game birds within. The classic crown wood* that we readily accept as the norm today is largely only the way it is thanks to the pheasant and the men who liked to shoot them. Hedges, in addition to those planted for enclosure, were added and then later laid to encourage them to grow taller, wider and thicker. The keepers knew better than anyone that a dense and towering hedgerow provided the best shelter for a nesting grey partridge, and healthy broods meant more birds, meaning more coveys in autumn, making driven partridge shooting possible. In the shooting season those same vast hedges acted as screens behind which the Guns would stand. The skeltering covey of wild greys would only see waiting Guns at the last minute, leading them to starburst out at all points of the compass. The same is true today: you'll not find a better hedge anywhere in Britain than on one of the precious few partridge manors that remain. The Duke of Norfolk's Peppering estate is a perfect example of

---

* Woods planted by people that look like a queen's crown: domed with thick spikier edges around the rim.

this clear understanding that the hedgerow is vital to lowland wildlife conservation. Before embarking on his concerted effort to return the grey partridge to the Sussex Downs, he first had his hedgerow network mapped. The management plan that ensued led to fourteen kilometres of new hedgerows planted and the existing hedges to undergo laying and coppicing to increase their overall biodiversity value. The duke puts much of the breeding success these Peppering partridges now enjoy down to the proliferation of hedgerow havens; of course this is allied equally with a dedicated team of gamekeepers, who ensure the sustained provision of food and targeted predator control.

The Wildlife Trusts estimate that 85 per cent of English heathland has disappeared in the past 150 years. Much of that which clung on, neither falling under the plough nor planted with commercial conifers, did so because it was maintained overwhelmingly for sport. This was particularly the case in the Breckland region of Suffolk and Norfolk. Why bother, asked the wealthy sporting landowners, men such as Lord Iveagh, the Duke of Grafton or Lord Walsingham, to attempt to make a scant return from farming such marginal land if it could hold partridge and pheasant instead? Scrub and furze and broom whips were heeled in and grew to make yet more cover. These pits of cover are still a significant feature of Norfolk, continuing to act as oases for game and wildlife within seas of de-stoned former heath that now grows vegetables.

That much of the landscape that we recognise as quintessential 'English countryside' looks the way it does is not solely due to the agricultural activities of those who owned the land, but is thanks to their sporting pastimes, namely shooting. This landscape can be understood through the medium of Thomas Gainsborough's painting *Mr and Mrs Andrews* (1750). Robert Andrews was a squire on the Essex side of the River Stour. Reportedly a devout agricultural improver, he is pictured by Gainsborough leaning against an oak tree, garbed in a baggy shooting coat with a gun crooked over his arm and pointer seated at heel. His wife Frances is also seated, yet, unlike the dog who looks up in adoration of his master, she stares assuredly at the viewer. Indeed, the Andrews both appear confidently content with their lot. Little wonder: the land in which they sit, they own; it appears healthy and fecund in both agrarian and sporting terms. The National Gallery, who are the custodians of the work, claim this is Gainsborough's most faithful representation of a landscape. He had no need to embellish or add any whistles and bells of artistic licence. In *Mr and Mrs Andrews* we are treated to a vision of a boom period in farming, the second agricultural revolution, as it was known, where farm outputs grew faster than the human population. The Stour Valley of the mid-1700s really was this lush, productive and mixed. The sheaves of wheat we see give evidence of rich arable; the sheep are plump, grazing in a meadow, fenced on one side by chestnut paling; on the other three sides are hedges, all of which have clearly been laid the previous winter. You can almost hear the pheasants crowing in a crown-shaped covert painted in the middle distance. The only missing element is the labourers like myself – we are there in our work but not in person. The absence of my forebears aside, this snapshot of Georgian splendour, of a place of sustainable farming, shooting and hunting, is poignant, particularly when compared with Constable's depressed Suffolk we see a mere half century or so later.

By the mid-nineteenth century the notion of walking about, getting tattered by briar and thorn, in the hope of sport soon became a thing to be looked down upon. It became thought of as the activity of rustics like Mr Andrews, not suitable at all for the new breed of debonair landowning classes. Mr Andrews had calluses on his hands, cleaned his own gun and minded his pennies. Discerning shots now thought it far better to stand at a peg, alongside a group of similarly lofty pals, and have pheasants driven towards them, *en battue*, as the French had it. A man's prowess was no longer judged on his ability to hold his port and march twenty miles in pursuit of a brace of pheasants, a hare and a partridge for the pot; instead the sport became about marksmanship and abundance. 'Sporting birds and plenty of 'em' was the key, according to the Marquess of Westminster. In 1825, the 1st Marquess began to rear pheasants to bolster the dwindling wild stocks on his Eaton Hall estate. In 1831, William IV passed the Game Act, which removed the qualification of property ownership for those wishing to shoot game. Now all you needed was a game licence and the landowner's permission. Shooting tenancies erupted, as did the rearing of game and levels of gun ownership. For the first time since King Harold took an arrow to the eye, 'John Bull' once more had the right to hunt in England (provided he had the money for a ticket). In the mid-1840s, thanks to the ever-trend-setting catalyst of royal patronage, driven game shooting had become the very pip of fashion. By the late 1800s game shooting had overtaken fox hunting as the most popular field sport. Whilst the countryside still had its fair share of rough-shooting Georgian throwbacks, driven game was now pre-eminent.

Game shooting, like any fashion, became bloated and ridiculous. Estates vied with their neighbours to produce larger and yet larger bags of birds for the Guns. If jolly King Edward VII came visiting, gross gluttony ensued. For example, in the year of Edward's coronation, the grand shooting estate of Elveden, the seat of Lord Iveagh in Breckland, recorded a total bag for the season of 22,071 pheasant and 4,393 partridges. At a glance these appear obscene numbers, yet does this reflect some sort of Edwardian ecocide? The matter-of-fact *Memoirs of a Gamekeeper* written by Tom Turner, who worked as a beat keeper, then head keeper, at Elveden carries an enlightening appendix largely, it must be said, on death. Tom's account, covering a career that stretched from 1869 to 1952, gives an insight into the grandeur of such estates. The lists of the 'vermin' he and his underkeepers killed annually are eye-watering. There were 10,489 rats accounted for in 1907 and 1,006 stoats in 1905. The account goes on to list all of the hedgehogs, weasels, corvids, hawks (he lumps all birds of prey into this category), foxes, squirrels, otters, and various other 'enemies' that were killed in order to preserve game birds – because Tom was a preserver, rather than the modern incarnation of gamekeeper/conservationist. While his appendix may appear to be a list of the slain, it is very much an account of the living too. He makes copious notes on the birds (other than partridges and pheasants) who called Elveden home. Tom writes of crossbills and wrynecks, corncrakes and shrikes, plovers and corn buntings, wheatears and stonechats; these along with ninety-four other bird species he records with a seeming nonchalance, not because he looked on them with disdain, but simply because they were all in commonplace profusion in his lifetime.

The Suffolk of Tom Turner's day was one that tweeted and buzzed and sang with wildlife, not in spite of his predator control and land management regime, but largely because of it. The 'game department' at Elveden was so powerful that it dictated what could – or could not – happen on the farm. A labourer would be tipped a sixpence for marking a grey partridge nest, pheasants four pence. Harvesting and mowing were conducted at times and in ways that would not endanger nesting pheasant or partridge. Field margins were, under his aegis, wide and wild, hedges were thick and tree-belts prolific. All of these actions were designed to protect game, but they did the same favour for lapwing, stone curlew and skylark. In his woods, the strict regime of 'keep out' was most certainly in place to prevent disturbance to the pheasants, yet this also ensured peace for the nightingales that nested in the scrub, and nightjars could whirr away to their heart's ease. Admittedly for predators, be they feathered or furred, Turner's Elveden was a dangerous place to be. But if you look at the figures from 1903 until Tom retired in 1953, the year-upon-year numbers he killed remain fairly consistent, as for that matter do the numbers of pheasants and partridges in the game larder; nothing was being wiped out or eradicated by his actions. Some might argue this highlights that a concerted lengthy and lethal campaign against predators is a pointless exercise. Yet, conversely, it is easily reasoned that this somewhat stuffy keeper's memoir evidences that if you are to have plentiful biodiversity, killing predators is an essential limb of the three-legged stool of conservation. However hard Tom tried, the best he could do was control, never eliminate, predatory animals and birds. Wildlife thrived and he ensured the farming complemented it by dictating when fields could be cut for hay or how a field was harvested or even what it was drilled with. Elveden, like all shooting estates up to the Second World War, epitomised the hunter's paradox. They were places set up so that fabulously wealthy people could shoot at gamebirds until their barrels grew too hot to the touch. Such estates were micro-managed, and they were totally reliant upon the vast wealth of the private landowner. Yet these gilded places were also, partly by happenstance and partly by design, places of unsurpassed, nature-rich abundance.

The modern incarnation of driven game shooting is notably different from anything Tom Turner would have recognised. Now largely gone are the rearing fields where keepers brooded pheasant eggs under bantams. No more are the wild stocks of pheasants and partridges jealously guarded and protected; farm workers receive no tip for spotting a partridge nest. The gin traps and pole traps Tom set are history, as is the array of poisons he would have used to kill birds of prey. The keeper no longer gets much, if any say, in farming practices on an estate. Largely gone, too, are the rich men who paid for the small army of keepers and warreners, woodsmen and hedgelayers, whose efforts ensured the estates were rich in habitat. Yet game shooting's greatest change since the Tom era is that it has morphed from a pastime enjoyed only by the niche mega-rich or throwback yeomen into a more democratised activity. The notion that a hedgelayer could have stood at a peg in tweeds in Tom's day would have seemed preposterous to him. I would at best have been given a place in his beating line, but to stand as a Gun? Ridiculous.

Democratising shooting has turned it into an industry. Not in its entirety, of course. There are still thousands of syndicates throughout Britain where eight or ten like-minded souls chip in an annual subscription to lease sporting rights and purchase a few hundred or, at a stretch, a few thousand pheasant or red-legged partridge poults. These folks frequently take on the role of gamekeeper themselves, and with the zealotry of the keen amateur they rear their birds, trap the predators and improve their woods. They plant cover crops and lean on farmers to leave corners rough and the margins wild. They carry out all of this invaluable conservation work to enjoy a few days' shooting each season, and the overall farm wildlife benefits from their actions. A survey by the land agents Lycetts concluded 43 per cent of all shoots in Britain are syndicates. There are also the countless farmer's shoots, private affairs, like at Flea Barn or Hainey Farm. The farm-wide conservation activities undertaken by these landowners have a double pay-off: the likes of Ed and Charles enjoy a day's shooting and delight in entertaining their friends, and, although the shoot provides them with no direct financial return, it gives a focus for their farmland conservation. The hunter's paradox shows its hand once again. There are of course a handful of private estates where things are still done on the grand scale with grand guests, admittedly with smaller bags than their Edwardian ancestors – places like Sandringham, Hilborough or Peppering. But these are scarce in the countryside of today. Many of these smart, landed seats still need to sell a day or two's shooting to help pay the bills. Little wonder: we live in a time where land is so highly priced and valued that it has to wash its own face financially, and this latter truth helped lead to shooting's true brush with industrialisation.

By the late 1980s landowners were encouraged by the government to diversify agricultural land use. Death duties and market crashes during the 1970s had led the landed gentry into a state of being land-rich yet cash-poor. If growing crops or rearing livestock didn't pay the bills, and your City investments brought scant returns, which were taxed to the hilt anyway, why not make your land work for you in a different way? Some built golf courses, others holiday villages and camp sites. Safari and theme parks, motorways and motor museums sprang up in the shadows of stately piles. More than a few cash-strapped grandees looked with a canny eye at the upstart yuppies, the new breed in the City, working sixteen-hour days and desperate to spend their money on hedonistic pleasures. If farm shoots and syndicates had democratised shooting for the old-school yokels, hedgelayers and yeomen, 'commercial shoots' did likewise for the new elite of Guns. Sporting agents appeared, selling shooting to hedge-fund managers, stockbrokers and bond traders, as if flogging a corporate day at Twickenham or Silverstone. Such days offered all the superficial trappings of a day on a ducal estate without your family name having to be included in Debretts. The agents showed their spreadsheets to estate owners. Column A highlighted the costs – the purchasing and rearing of poults, the planting of maize to create drives, the feed bills, staff wages, shoot-day expenses of beaters, pickers-up and hospitality. Column B showed the income, and it was a figure with decent returns. It didn't take an arch genius to work out that the more birds put in the bag, the greater the income: the costs remained more or less the same, but the profits increased dramatically. In 2022, a team of eight Guns buying a day's shooting paid an average of £46 for every pheasant and £44 for each partridge they shot. Far better then, for the agents and their clients, that the Guns shoot 200 or 300 birds in a day than half that number. Of course, if you want to really reap the financial rewards, you need to host as many days' shooting as possible, not to mention release the corresponding number of pheasants. Lycetts estimate that a mere 11 per cent of shoots are run to make a profit.

Many of these commercial ventures are sustainable, well run and provide biodiversity net gain, just as the syndicates, farmers' shoots and grand old estates do. Some, however, do not. Rod Hazell, the gamekeeper at Frostenden in the Sandlings, once told me: 'The problem with shooting these days is that people are making money out of something that was never supposed to be profitable.' The commercialisation of shooting has led in some parts of Britain to overstocking of pheasants in release pens. This leads to the near destruction of woods, denuding the understorey and decimating invertebrate life, leaving them places of sterility for years to come. Levels of disturbance from repeated days' shooting place intolerable pressures upon wildlife. Rats, corvids and foxes abound, due to the sheer scale of birds and the supplementary feeding that is required to hold such a number. The end product, the thousands of shot pheasants and partridges, has a limited market – the British palate is just not that into the taste of game meat. At best the carcass may make its way into a Greggs sausage roll; more likely it will become dog food. There are valid arguments that these shoots are vital to hard-pressed rural economies, providing much-needed income for hospitality businesses and employment for keepers, beaters and pickers-up. Yet what price these jobs? The – admittedly small – number of commercial shoots that have intensified their operations to environmentally unsustainable levels are as destructive to the countryside as the farmers who have worked their soils to dust, treating the land like there is no tomorrow. Equally they have helped to tar everybody who shoots with their own grimy brush. When Tom Turner retired as Elveden's head keeper in 1953, his fame, and the high regard in which he was held as a rural custodian and naturalist, were such that Anglia Television dedicated an entire programme to his life and thoughts. Today, it appears that anyone who professes a penchant for a day's shooting is classed by wider society as 'worse than Hitler', mainly thanks to the perception that all game shooting is the unsustainable excesses seen on some commercial shoots.

There is of course a somewhat simple answer to stopping the gross excesses of such enterprises. Licensing the 11 per cent of shoots in Britain that are commercially run is only fair; after all, if you want to work in a particular industry you have to accept the statutes and regulations that accompany all industrialisation. Yet this notion is treated with horror by the organisations who run shooting, and unsurprisingly the commercial shoots themselves. 'The thin end of the wedge for an overall ban,' they say. Tom, I am sure, would have hated these 'commercial boys'; I know Darren hates them, which is why he refuses to sell them his stock.

A game farmer is little different from any other sort of livestock farmer. Darren sells fertile eggs for others to hatch and rear on, or chicks, all yellow and chocolate brown, which will be placed in brooder huts under lamps to grow into poults. The poults he sells are for the more risk-averse or time-poor individuals. Whatever the rearing regime may be, ultimately the poults will go into a release pen. These are fenced-off areas, either within a wood or scrub block for pheasants or in more open cover for partridges. It amuses Darren, in a somewhat head-shaking manner, that those who find the notion of reared-pheasant shooting abhorrent find few qualms with eating chicken – be it free range or kept in a barn. 'Those chicks are only going one way,' he says, nodding in the direction of the huge Cranswick Foods slaughterhouse and processing factory that looms near his rearing fields. 'At least my pheasants have got two chances,' he adds. It is true that a pheasant or partridge does lead a wilder, healthier and more natural life than any domesticated eating bird. A game bird may well avoid the Guns on a shoot day and live to fly another day; if not, and a dose of Number 6 shot ends his life, he is no more or less dead than the chicken or turkey on the production line at the abattoir.

Looking back at my diaries, they reveal 70 per cent of our hedging work is undertaken on farms and estates where game shooting takes place in some form or other. This comes as little surprise. Pheasants may not be such expensive items when Darren sells them as eggs, chicks or poults, but they are worth a lot when it comes to the time for them to be flushed over the Guns. There is an Edwardian era *Punch* cartoon about the cycle of pheasant economics. It runs: 'up goes a guinea, off goes a penny farthing and down comes two and six'. It's aged due to decimalisation and inflation, but highlights that the pheasant then, as now, is only valuable when it takes to the wing on a shooting day. So ensuring your game is well catered for is not only good stockmanship; it also makes complete commercial sense. The hedgerow is essential for game. Pheasants roost in woods, but during daylight hours they range out across open farmland, feeding on seeds, greenery and insects. Pheasants and partridges are fairly straightforward creatures. They, like all birds, require three fundamentals to thrive: a plentiful supply of their preferred foodstuffs, which the hedge provides; some level of protection from predators, again supplied by a dense hedgerow; and the right sort of habitat in which to raise young, which the hedge also furnishes. Hen pheasants and partridges lay their clutches in the immediate lee of hedgerows within clumps of tussock grass. It would be true to say that the gamekeeper prizes a thick, well-managed hedge to a far greater degree than any farmer.

Game birds feed themselves partly with the help of man. Known as supplementary feeding, wheat is either placed in static feeders, or keepers 'spin' food by hand or in a contraption affixed to the back of a quad bike. Additionally, many of the seed-bearing crops specifically sown on farms for birds also provide food for game. As far as predator control goes, the reared pheasant is fairly fortunate. Once out of its poult phase, most English birds of prey, bar the frankly psychotic goshawk, find the 'long tail' too much of a handful. All corvids delight in raiding a wild-pheasant or -partridge nest, taking egg or chick with impunity. But the reared adult game bird is a step too far, even for a raven to bother with. The fox is a clear and present danger, and keepers take great efforts to suppress this threat, largely by shooting at night and through the use of snares. Stoats, weasels, rats and grey squirrels are also predators, of nests rather than of fully grown birds, so whilst these may be controlled by reared-bird gamekeepers, it is to a notably lesser degree than their counterparts on wild-bird shoots. As for habitat for pheasants and partridges, the simple truth is the overwhelming majority of the hedgelaying and coppicing that Gouldy and I do each season is carried out with game in mind. It would be wrong to say that farmers who shoot are the only agrarians who care about the wildlife on their farms, but clearly, in our case, most of our customers are driven to greater levels because of the game bird. It seems to me that the ready willingness of politicians, campaigners and many wildlife charities to denigrate and seek to end reared-game shooting because of the repulsive greed and woeful practices of a handful of commercial enterprises is not only narrow minded, but, worse still, ultimately bad for wildlife.

In a countryside that is increasingly pressured to grow more food for less, to have more houses and infrastructure built upon it, a landscape that is criss-crossed by roads filled with more and yet more cars, with lay-bys desecrated with fly-tipped rubbish, with rivers and ponds polluted, it is all too clear that active custodians of land for wildlife are desperately needed. A question worth pondering: would my order book for hedgerow management jobs be so filled if game shooting were curtailed or banned? Would the sporting farmers and landowners be so inclined to pay Gouldy and me to lay their hedges if partridges were no longer flushed over them? Would they pay our invoices for managing their woods, creating rides, and replanting and guarding 'regen' saplings? Would they plant tens of thousands of acres of cover crops and seed crops and improve their margins if they could no longer shoot the pheasants that live within them? Would they bother with the costs and hassle of supplementary feeding? Would they trap the carrion crows or shoot the foxes if they could no longer treat their friends to a day's shooting?

The role of hedgerows in rural landscapes has shifted. No longer are they primarily used to fence in livestock or shelter crops. Instead, they are prized as a place of biodiversity, habitat and food provision. This modern function is of utmost importance to the shooting fraternity. For the gamekeeper, quality cover, nesting habitat and abundant insect life are keys to success, particularly for those who rely solely or partly on wild game birds to fill the bag. Game shooting is undergoing something of a revolution. There is an obvious waning in demand for quantity, which requires mass releases of reared pheasants and partridges. The trend is shifting towards quality. Reared birds are no longer a cheap mass-market commodity, released with seemingly scant regard for the wider environment. Wild broods are now cherished and therefore closer attention is being paid to the three-legged stool of conservation to cater for them. Shooting is returning to something that the eighteenth-century Essex squire Robert Andrews would have understood. This shift is unsurprising, simply reflecting the wholesale movement towards sustainable methods of farming and rural land management. Our hedgerows are havens for game and wildlife. That both farmers and gamekeepers now see a discernible environmental and financial value in their health and vitality bodes well for their future.

8

Flailing About

I lean on a hedging stake and watch John at work in his digger, seated behind his scratched and dusty screen. John works for the Barkers. They are farmers – conservation-minded farmers – who have been presented with many awards for their efforts. John's eyes glitter like those of a stoat hunting: intent, intelligent, alert. He is wearing grimy overalls, a Fendt logo on the breast pocket, betraying his favourite breed of contemporary draught horse. He is slouched and his body is twisted. To my thinking the ergonomic seat in his cab was designed for a fatter man. I see his hands too. His left operates levers next to his knees. His right holds a joystick, long oily fingers pluck and pull and flick at unseen buttons with the speed and dexterity of a Spanish guitarist, and then the tree shear rears out. The cutting tool, at the business end, is shaped like an adder's head, the jaws open, ready to strike. The head of the snake revolves ninety degrees in a hiss of oil, and the mouth opens wider still, exposing twin blades.

The tree shear acts like a gardener's set of secateurs, but John's kit is no horticulturalist's tool. It is hydraulic-powered and monstrous. The now-open maw has one blunt, anvil-like blade; the other is sharp. John twiddles with levers and the digger's strong arm thrusts into the hedge, the fangs closing around the trunk of a hawthorn. It cracks, squeezes, then crushes with a sound like a boot on an ice-filled puddle. John presses a foot pedal and the cab pirouettes 180 degrees to drop a brashy branch of coppiced thorn behind him, joining a row containing hundreds more decapitated hedge plants: thorn, guelder rose, maple and spindle. With his heel John commands his vehicle to advance. It responds with a trundle and jerks ten metres to the left, rolling across the sodden February field. With the slightest of jolts he halts, then repeats.

It might sound unromantic, all that metal and noise, but I could watch John all day. There is beauty in the way he uses this kit and there is harmony in the way we work together. I pump the rubberised globe of the primer on my chainsaw, flushing fuel into the carb of the engine. Safety bar forward, choke engaged, right hand on the pull cord. The compact Japanese engine coughs. Choke off, and at the second pull the saw starts. I rev the saw to full bore for five seconds. Gouldy always laughs at this piece of high-tech micro-engineering. 'Fisher Price kit', he calls it. Anything but a Stihl is a toy in his regard. But I continue to marvel at something so small being able to produce so much power.

Chain-brake forward, the engine roars like one of those boys in their hatchbacks giving it hell down the A12 near Lowestoft on a dark winter's night. I approach the line of tattered stems where, before John and his digger got going, a hedge, open and sparse in the base, had stood, no good for anything much, certainly not for wildlife. I stoop and start cutting.

Brake off, throttle squeeze, engine roar and the saw's chain of forty-seven links of shark-like teeth becomes an instant blur in a spray of bar oil and chemical reek from the Aspen fuel. With a right-to-left cut, I tidy a coppiced stem, the tear and tatter left by the tree shear now cut clean, the gobbet of hawthorn removed, angled, sliced at an approximate thirty degrees. The open wound faces the south-east so that winter winds can dry it. When the sap returns in a month or so, the early sun will summon the return of life and the buds will erupt in claret pustules. In short order, as spring evolves, these buds burst and become juvenile stems, drawing their power and vitality from the combination of the sun and the long-established roots of the mother plant that delve and spread deep into the Suffolk clay. Where once a single stem had been, the now coppiced stool will be a home to many. I repeat the process on every limb that John and his digger have raggedly munched, leaving one trunk, every two paces or so, cut at three feet high. The rest I trim to ground level. Once John's shear and my saw have finished cutting along the entire half-kilometre length, he will remove the snake's head and replace it with a grab. His tracks will retrace their rolling steps, and the cab will spin, and the boom will flex and bend, picking up the brash and placing it around the newly coppiced hedge, pushing it in firmly to cover the clean-snicked hedge stools. The taller pollards will retain the whole in what is known as a dead hedge. Yet this line of twigs and thorn and desiccated berry is very much alive; it is the dead protecting the new. I look round to see that John's tracks are trundling again – we have an hour yet, and at least 200 more cuts to make, before we stop for lunch.

I LEARNED TO LAY hedges in a place where hedges were once king. Quenby Hall stands proud, perched atop a ha-ha at Leicestershire's highest point. The towers of mellowed chequer-board brick provide a focal point for the estate, the 'Taj Mahal of the grass country', as one *Horse and Hound* correspondent described it in the early twentieth century. The term grass country is a fairly self-explanatory piece of hunting parlance, meaning a terrain of old turf, a land almost devoid of arable. This part of the East Midlands has been under grass for so long it's as if, in a half-hearted attempt to mask the agricultural ways of the Middle Ages, the Enclosure Movement manifested itself by spreading a gossamer blanket of green over the ridge and furrow left by ploughmen and their oxen. The ridge and furrow, still clearly visible today under the green sward, acts as a reminder that the only permanent features in the English countryside are formed by humans and our farming. In my time in the Shires these tracts of rippling agricultural antiquity were a mundane part of life, something of a pest in truth, causing the horses to stumble when I galloped over them or creating seasick nausea as I piloted a tractor pulling a Cambridge roller or chain harrow in order to refresh the grass that my nags ate in summer.

The estate was then owned by Squire De Lisle, known as Gerald to his peers, 'Squire' to the rest of us. He was the most remarkable of men. If a novelist had faithfully painted his description, critics would either argue that the writer was a plagiarist, surely knocking off Wodehouse, or suggest such a character was too perfectly minorly aristocratic and bonkers to be remotely believable. That is not to say the Squire was stupid or affected. He was well read and well lived and could chat on nearly any subject. A staunch Catholic, he had never wholly forgiven England for the regicide of Charles I; a devout countryman, it confused him that some could so violently despise hunting. Hunting, after all, to him was just as much a part of the land as his acres of rolling grass, the cattle in the park or the foxes he so wholeheartedly protected (unless it was a hunting Friday). A conservative to his core, he was a liberal soul for all that. As a landlord he was easygoing and as a human being a delight. He set the tone for the whole estate. On rare occasions the squire would take me to one side, look me in the eye and say, 'Not quite up to our standards today, Richard,' in mild admonishment for some dereliction of tidiness or professionalism. After this most understated of bollockings, he would smile, revealing a notably fine set of teeth, then turn on his heel, confident that his point had been made and understood. My staff and I, the moment his well-shone boots clicked and clacked out of the stable yard, would pick up brooms and begin to sweep; his lofty standards osmotically became our standards too. His ways imbued in us a more ancient mindset, one that was admittedly out of kilter with much of the late-twentieth-century world outside the boundaries of the estate.

For those who have never experienced life on an old estate like this, it is difficult to comprehend its ethos and character. To an outsider, seeing an old toff like De Lisle being deferentially addressed by his tenantry with a doffed cap and a 'Morning, Squire' would appear at best a pastiche – a multiple-act play, put on largely for the entertainment of the principal player. At worst, the onlooker might believe he was witnessing a terrible and hierarchical case of 'us and them', of lords and laymen, of haves and have-nots. How ghastly, they would say: he has all this, yet the staff (and the bloke who rents the stables) are nothing but bonded serfs; they own nought but the boots they stand up in, and they're full of holes.

Yet this was so far from the truth. Estate life is unlike town life; unlike village life, even. An estate is a hive, with each member of that hive utterly reliant upon the other. The sum of the parts makes the whole. The squire was the squire, his oldest son Freddie the heir apparent. The gardener did the gardening, the lodge keeper put the chain across the drive. Malcos the Peruvian houseman did the indoor male things, his wife Flora did the indoor female things. Vivian Dixon the housekeeper kept the house. I messed about with the horses. The squire's wife, Edith, or 'Madam' as we called her, arguably truly ran things as such ladies tend to do. Then there was Michael, Vivian's husband.

If you were to bottle Quenby, then distil it, then repeat this several times more, so that it was refined to such perfection as to be in its purest possible form, it would not be essence of De

Lisle, nor Sir Harold Nutting (the pre-De Lisle master of Quenby). It wouldn't be the Ashbys, the piratical slavers who built the original hall in 1562, not even the abbot, monks and assorted clerics who had lived there quite happily when the oxen ploughed the ridges and furrows until Henry VIII messed it all up for them, smashing their cloisters and grabbing their assets in order to replace his old Spanish wife with a new one from Norfolk. No, the quintessential Quenbyness of Quenby could only be found in the form of Michael Dixon. Michael taught me how to lay hedges.

When Michael set off hedging he did so alone, bar his Border collie Meg. I'd catch sight of him each morning as I dismounted from exercising some young horse or other. He'd trundle by the stables in his steady, considered way, seated in a scrupulously cleaned Ford tractor, Meg's lithe black and white frame curled tight in the footwell. Behind the chugging beast he pulled a trailer, constructed to his own very specific requirements. Originally a muck spreader, the Heath Robinson-style contraption now held stakes and binders and string and rails and rolls of savage wire. A place was artfully created for his chainsaw and hammer. His billhook – 'me most important tool', as he repeatedly told me – was well cosseted on a shelf of its own, wrapped in an old and oily spud sack. Shining new staples and nails lived in boxes, alongside which rested a home-welded device for removing the old ones. Every tool, gadget and gewgaw he carried had a purpose, each had a specific drawer, shelf or hook within the Dixon fencing trailer, with only Michael knowing its exact location. As he rattled and jingled out of sight, drumming across the cattle grid, I would watch him and run up my stirrups, vowing, 'I'll go and catch up with him once I've lunged that new grey horse.'

It took no little effort for me to persuade Michael to reveal his hedging secrets. This was not due to some fear that I might usurp his position. After all, in an estate hive each drone has his own specific job. His was the fencing, mine the nags, therefore there was no potential for a demarcation dispute. Michael was reluctant because he was a worrier. He worried and wobbled about many things. He feared the horses might get colic in my absence, he feared I might chop off my leg with a saw, he feared I might chop off his leg with a saw. He fretted that the slash I made on a pleacher would be of insufficient quality, he dreaded the words from the guvnor, 'Not quite up to our standards, Michael.' After a year or so of my nagging, Michael let me loose. He showed me the angles to cut and what brash to leave and what to keep. He'd take a stake I had placed and move it to just the right point so that it was of full use. He showed me the old ways, like how to bind and when to bind, and he showed me the new ways, guarding his finished work with a taut strand of barbed wire so that munching cattle belonging to Mr Barnacle, the wonderfully archaic tenant who ran his beasts on my side of the estate, would not browse our handiwork to sticks.

One day I accompanied Michael to the national hedgelaying championships, held that year on a neighbouring estate. We watched the old lads and young lads at their work. The majority laying Midland-style, pleachers clean on the ditch side, brashy on the far, in order to protect their immaculate efforts from the later attentions of cattle. Others adopted the South of England style, double brushed and centrally staked, done so that sheep could graze on either side of the hedgerow after laying. The Derbyshire layers worked to suit the needs of their terrain, shunning binders and choosing heavier pleachers accordingly. Yorkshiremen, with belt and braces, backed up their lowly laid pleachers with post and rail. A handful of West Country and Montgomeryshire hedgers tried to recreate their methods for the judges, nearly impossible in the Shires: back home they worked atop earthen banks, a phenomenon never seen in this grass country. Michael and I met up with a cabal of his pals, who accepted my presence with the ready openness that epitomises the country people of the East Midlands. We smoked fags and drank carrot-coloured tea out of polystyrene cups. The throng in their boilersuits discussed the standards of work and laughed fully at jokes I half understood. 'What style do you call your hedges then, Michael?' I asked, having seen nothing in this competition that wholly resembled my mentor's own work. 'Me own,' he replied in a fug of Lambert and Butler. Michael Dixon had laid hedges for the best part of half a century when I met him, after which time he had concluded that the job hinges on practicality, not craft for craft's sake. Of all the gifts Michael gave me, the greatest was an understanding that practicality and pragmatism go a long way in managing hedges, and for that matter almost any other wildlife habitat. It is only nearly thirty years later that I realise so much of the ethos in hedgerow management that I call my own was in truth pilfered from the wobbling, worrying, wondrous Michael Dixon. The actions Gouldy and I take are based on an amalgam of what is good for the hedge, good for the farm, good for wildlife and financially good for him and me. If any of these factors are missing, then hedgerow management is unsustainable.

Using a 360-digger-mounted tree shear to take on the donkey work of coppicing follows these four maxims of sustainable hedgerow management. The hydraulic ram of the digger is capable of feats that a man with an axe or a saw could only dream of. Yet the digger with its oil-under-pressure-powered blades should not work in isolation. A tree shear cuts with a ragged bite; the result is dramatic, savagely and economically effective, but the cracks, splits and tears it leaves on the stool allow in the rain, rot creeps downwards and the hoped-for multi-stems never appear. Instead all that flushes is weak and spindly. Worse still, an overly battered hedge with rotting stumps and shaken roots simply gives up and dies. A tidying cut with a chainsaw prevents this, and if you make that slice at an angle so the rain runs off and the cut faces the sun, then the coppiced hedge has all it needs for regrowth to occur.

The concept of dead hedging – protecting the new growth with the pruning material – over coppiced hedgerows was an idea borne out of both contemporary practical necessity and ancient ways. Ancient, in that dead hedging has been the woodland coppicer's means of protecting and forming coups since man first discovered that some species of tree will successfully coppice. Practical, because in deer-filled East Anglia, the zesty new growth that springs up on hedgerows after coppicing becomes food for the muntjac and roe. If this basal herbage is nibbled and browsed repeatedly, the hedge will die, its energy all gone. The brown hares that proliferate join in the assault, and there are a lot of them: the conservation efforts on Suffolk and Norfolk farms that focused on returning the grey partridge from the brink of extinction are equally beneficial for hares. In our large East Anglian fields ringed by hedges and floristic margins, the brown hare laughs in the face of the perceived notion that they are rare. These wild-eyed fidgety creatures live more than ten to the acre on many farms; they nip the shoots of thorn, guelder and maple with a scissor-clean bite. The dead hedging that John grasped in the grab on his digger provides a defence for the coppiced hedge against this onslaught of teeth. While the brash is not a complete answer, it markedly lessens the effect of browsing by wildlife; in effect it shares the bounty between farmer and nature. The dead hedge also provides a latticework of support for the regrowing stems, through which they writhe upwards towards the light, in much the manner that a gardener places supports made of arty rusted metal or rustic hazel woven around the base of a heavy-headed rose. As the dead hedge rots down, the invertebrates, in the hedgerow bottom, feed and breed in the decaying detritus, and insect-eating birds delight in the easy pickings. The hedgehogs, voles and shrews scurry and watch for predators. The starkness of hedgerow coppicing during the period of regrowth is dramatically lessened for all wildlife. The hedge itself, meanwhile, does what hedges do and erupts back into frenzied life, energised into dramatic reaction by this intervention of cutting, guarded in its shroud of old limbs.

Hedgelaying only works – producing a hedge with vigorous dense regrowth from base to tip – because of the reaction shrubby hedgerow plant species have to being coppiced. Laying hedges is in essence coppicing on steroids. There is the basal eruption at the cut heel, and a similar occurrence along the lateral length of the laid pleacher: each node along the limb laid at forty degrees produces countless buds that then shoot and grow upwards to the sun. The original purpose of hedgelaying was to utilise this natural phenomenon and fill gaps, thickening the whole to make a stock-proof barrier. Today this notion of stock proofing is utterly redundant, certainly in the arable lands of East Anglia. Yet we still lay hedges, because we fully understand the benefits for wildlife that laying provides. It is ultimately worth the slow toil, scratches, insect bites, backache and looming risk of chopping a limb off. The obvious question is, why not then stick solely to laying and shun the shear and saw of coppicing? Why leave fields nearly hedgeless for a year, maybe two, while they regrow, with mere lines of dead brash covering the severed stools?

First, a hedge that is so overgrown and so decrepit that it has become nigh-on a linear wood, with hawthorn hollowed by age, maple as thick as a tree and blackthorn suckered into a tunnel, would be a menace to lay, most probably a failure with broken limbs all round. Far better, therefore, to coppice this monster and let the ancient roots once more bear witness to new life. Second, time is money in farming; the same is true in practical conservation. If we accept the unquestionable truth that hedges must, in roughly twenty-year cycles, endure significant interventionist management in order that they continue to exist as hedgerows, then the modern-day economics and practicalities of land management cannot be ignored. Gouldy and I can lay approximately fifty metres of hedge each day using the conservation style, ten to fifteen metres less if we are staking and binding, provided of course we are working on what we term a 'boy's hedge', this being a more recently planted hedge without an abundance of invasive bramble, old man's beard and briony. Equally, if the length is sited on a precipitous bank or teeters over a chasm-like ditch, then the process of clearing and singling, then laying, slows to a crawl, as does our daily rate of advance. Older, thickened limbs take feats of engineering to lay: multiple artful slices of the saw straighten the line to create wondrously thick hedges, but such work sucks dry any potential for profit. Our modernised hedgelaying is the epitome of wildlife conservation, but craft does not pay our bills. We are professional practical conservationists, enjoying no subsidy by charitable donation, nor resourced by flocks of volunteers. The brutal tree shear may shatter the illusion of old-world charm engendered by the image of a hedgelayer working steadily away with hook and beadle, but this is the truth of our work: we are on the clock. Yes, we are trying to save nature, but we have mortgages to pay too.

To maintain and improve a hedge, post laying or coppicing, means trimming. Pre-Second World War, hedgers used hand tools, invariably a 'slasher', which looked much like a spar hook attached to an over-length axe handle. With this tool, the side growth and bushy tops of the flourishing hedge were kept in check using multiple upward slashes; a flip of the wrist and the top was trimmed too. The sheer human mechanics of trimming with a slasher caused the hedge to form an 'A' frame, each tendril and branchlet, so cut, tillered out, emulating a coppiced hedge in miniature. Hedges trimmed to an 'A' expose more surface area to the sun, more daylight brings better growth, better growth is denser growth, denser growth means secure livestock. Ecologically, such a shape happens to offer more habitat variety for wildlife. Of course, the old boys wielding their slashers had no notion they were improving habitats; farming practices then did so by happenstance, not design. A hedge left untrimmed for three or four seasons begins the process of becoming a line of trees once more. The limbs thicken from twiggy, to stem and then trunk; the fruit moves to the outer extremities. The base becomes bare due to shading; the hedge starts to lose its hedginess. Hedge trimming by hand was a time-consuming job, one carried out by the men on the farm in winter once the work of tillage had been completed. The hedger on the slasher would be accompanied by at least one other worker, usually two, whose job it was to remove the cut brash from the margin and ditch, then pile it into bundles; any cordwood was retained to fuel their fires at home. The first job each morning was to set light to the brash piles of yesterday; if they were lucky the embers would still warm them at snap time.

There is a film called *Hedging* held in the archives of the BFI. Made in 1942 by the Realist Film Unit for the Ministry of Agriculture, the star of the show is Dyton, a Northamptonshire hedger, sporting a trilby and buskins, a pipe permanently dangling from his mouth. Dyton shows the audience his method of laying, staking and binding a straggly, gappy hedge in leafless midwinter. The landscape around him looks much like the one I knew at Quenby: old grass, waves of ridge and furrow; the ditch on which he stands is gentle, obviously hand-cut unlike the machined chasms I fall into today in Suffolk. His apprentice is a fresh-faced Land Girl, seemingly chosen not only for her attractive outdoorsiness – perfect for a recruitment drive for the Women's Land Army – but also for her work ethic. While Dyton deftly wields an unfeasibly sharp bill, the unnamed Land Girl in dungarees and gumboots is busy with her slasher, seemingly oblivious to the bramble and briar that snags at her unprotected face and curly bob. She clears out the brash and dead wood, leaving only the living pleachers for Dyton to lay.

In the *de rigeur* style of war-time infotainment, the camera operator delights in framing his subjects against the skyline in artful silhouette, while a clarinettist plays. This blending of sound and sight suits Dyton and his laid hedge, the director using him and his craft to represent an idyll worth fighting for, a place worth protecting. I wonder if the symbolism meant that much at all to a Bermondsey mother clutching a child to her breast and sheltering under her kitchen table as Luftwaffe bombs turned her street to rubble?

Dyton's laid hedge is nearly identical to the ones Michael Dixon produced: no competition-winner for sure, just pragmatic and practical. *Hedging* concludes with a two-minute jump to the ongoing maintenance of hedges. The narrator, in clipped BBC English, notes that it will be twenty years until the laid hedge needs Dyton's measured billhook strokes again; 'it will,' he adds as a caution, 'need regular trimming'. The film concludes with a clip of Dyton at work with his slasher, working a full mile length, trimming a hedge to an 'A' while the clarinet plays, now with the addition of strings. Once the camera stopped rolling and the men from the ministry went back to London, I imagine the forced grin on Dyton's gaunt face swiftly disappeared. The music, the narration and artful angles told a lie. Dyton's job was a bloody tough one, a task of thorny, poorly paid monotony. His daily reality was one of hardship and physicality, a near unimaginable world for today's office workers and work-from-homers.

Six years after *Hedging* appeared in cinemas, a Scottish farmer named Gilmour invented a tractor-mounted hedge cutter. He sold the manufacturing rights to a small Worcestershire-based agricultural engineering company called McConnel, who had already made a name for themselves producing high-quality trailers and fruit graders. The Mid-Mount Mark 1 was launched at the 1948 Royal Show. From this point on, the slasher became obsolete and, in truth, the Mid-Mount Mark 1 largely sang the death knell for men like Dyton too. The hedge cutter, also working under aliases such as a flail, jungle basher, brash cutter or bush whacker, is a remarkable tool, without doubt one of the few inventions which, along with Jethro Tull's horse-drawn hoe, revolutionised not only British farming but our entire landscape, for ever.

This was a machine, the advertising brochures boasted, that could carry out the work of eight men (saving £7 in wages per day, it added, by way of attracting cost-conscious potential buyers). Operators of the Mark 1 needed only to nose their tractor onto one side of the hedgerow, switch on the engine affixed to the loader arms, and set the cutters whirring. The flails trimmed and shaped brash, suckering stems and branches. The Mark 1 also cleaned ditches, dykes and margins of weed ingress, bramble and dead matter. If the job necessitated heavier-duty arboriculture, the head could be removed and replaced by a serrated disk, roughly the diameter of a round bale of hay. Once rotating, this head, like one of Wile E. Coyote's gadgets designed to kill Roadrunner, could cut through stumps and limbs up to five inches thick. The McConnel was capable of feats no man could hope to achieve with hand tools, and at a work rate that changed the slow, cyclical management of hedgerows and ditches that had previously been the steady grind of a farmer's winter work programme. No more would a hedger need to trudge a mile or more, billhook in his knapsack and a stringed faggot of stakes on his shoulder to undertake laborious, time- and cash-sapping toil. No longer was a full day's work entirely dependent on the weather or the strength of a human arm. No more would the old artisan be accompanied by the back'us boy, bearing the lunch bag and a slasher sloped over his shoulder, like a child soldier of the fifteenth century (every East Anglian farm had a back'us boy, who lived and worked in the back of the house, a lad of all jobs, usually the most unpleasant, scratchy, dirty or menial). No more did the hedge need to be manhandled at a man-handling pace. The flail ended the up-close-and-personal relationship of man with hedge.

As with all things in agricultural engineering, the innovation and refinement of hedge cutters went on apace. Less than fifteen years after the McConnel Mark 1's launch, Tony Turner, an engineer from Alcester in Warwickshire, patented a hydraulic-powered hedge cutter. Every flail since then has adapted and adopted the Turner system – a rear-mounted machine with a rotating cutter-head fixed on a telescopic boom. Over the decades the heads have developed, growing bigger, sharper, more powerful: the modern flail now boasts all of the dexterity and deftness of Dyton and his slasher, yet allied with the almost unimaginable grunt that modern engineering can conjure. The flail does of course still rely upon man, yet the man is shielded from thorn and wild wind, shielded from nature, secure and dry and safe in a tractor cab, twiddling his levers just as John does in his digger with a tree shear.

Flailing hedges wins farmers no friends. The flail seems to stand proxy as witness A for the prosecution, the charge being that farmers hate nature, hate wildlife and hate us. Every autumn after harvest, hedge cutters are hitched to tractors, and as the flails start to spin, in their wake spills a spew of tweets, posts and Instagram reels. These missives picture some nameless operator sporting overalls, seated in a cab with his neck craned chin-over-shoulder as he works away with his tractor and flail down a hedge. Invariably the scenes are snapped on some country road or public footpath – after all, there is no right to roam in England.

To be fair, the flail is indeed a brutal bit of kit, yet that is what the flail is, merely a bit of kit, no different from any other bit of kit that makes our life simpler, cheaper, more cost effective and more profitable. Gilmour designed the flail as a tool for trimming, the notion being that his machine could do what Dyton's slasher could do, just more of it and for less money.

The flail's design is adept at trimming growth up to about two inches thick; any more than that and the limbs shatter. The hedges that those who wander country lanes see being flailed so regularly and wholeheartedly are not being cut through some landowner-led obsession with neatness and order, nor are the farmers embarking on any sadistic campaign against the hedge, its denizens or the people who want to watch wildlife. The flail crunches its way along roads and paths through necessity. Public roadside and footpath hedges are cut to enable the passage of traffic, be that four wheeled, two wheeled, four legged or two legged. If the farmer doesn't cut these hedges, the council will. It is the local authority that is responsible for public safety and while a vast shaggy hedge delights a bullfinch, such a hedgerow turns a rural road into a deathly tunnel, with unseen dangers racing towards you at every turn. In 2021, NFU Mutual reported, the instances of traffic fatalities were 70 per cent higher on rural roads than on their urban equivalents. An overhanging hedge, causing blind spots on bends, gateways and field entrances on a twisting rural lane is a real and present danger, and with over 40 million cars on the road, a danger that year upon year grows greater. The landowner is also responsible for keeping footpaths and bridleways clear. By law vegetation must be cut back so that a footpath is a minimum of one and a half metres wide, a bridleway three metres. Fail to do so and not only are a farmer's BPS payment and grants under stewardship put at risk, but also he or she will fall foul of cross-compliance legislation and the Public Rights of Way Act, all of which spells a court case and a hefty fine. More practically, why would a farmer burn diesel, pay wages on human resource, and bear the costs of wear and tear on a machine costing over £20,000 (a McConnel 80-series machine retails at around £25,000 plus VAT) solely to partake in a destructive act that brings a financial return of zero? Farmers may be many things, but they are neither mindless vandals, nor do they like to spend money for no return. The truth is, the regular and seemingly brutal flailing that drivers and walkers witness, and then post on social media, is not done through any landowner devilment, but rather mundanely to abide by the law, prevent road traffic accidents and enable access to footpaths for the general public. Little wonder farmers hate the hedge-cutting season.

There is another good reason for regular cutting of roadside hedgerows, which is that it saves wildlife. In our management plans we never recommend a hedge adjacent to a road is managed specifically as wildlife habitat. Vehicle collisions are one of the main causes of mortality in Britain's wild mammals and birds. Project Splatter, a citizen science project led by Amy Schwartz and Sarah Raymond, collated roadkill recordings sent in by social media users. Between 2014 and 2019, 54,000 wildlife road deaths were reported. From foxes to muntjac, badgers to hedgehogs, pheasants to polecats and all points in between, these animals and birds were listed as falling victim to the onrushing wheels of cars, vans and lorries. Obviously this number is a fraction of the national figures for wildlife killed by vehicles. All of these wildlife species use hedgerow networks as causeways for travel, either within, over or alongside. Any conservationist, naturalist or rationalist would agree it is wholeheartedly counterproductive, indeed callous, to encourage nature into what is essentially a killing zone. Gouldy and I advocate cutting roadside hedgerows tight and trimming roadside verges. The main purpose for these hedgerows is as a barrier against snow drifts, preventing soil erosion and filtering chemical and nitrate runoff into water courses. A good roadside hedge is one that is an inhospitable place for wildlife.

Away from the roads and footpaths, the flail, used in the manner for which it was designed, is a hedgerow conservationist's ally. The flail encourages a hedge, after laying or coppicing, to tighten up and tiller into a dense and forbidding wall of thorn. It is true that some fruit will be lost, but not all; indeed, fruits such as the 'pomes' of hawthorn, sloes of blackthorn, hips of dog rose and berries of dogwood all appear on last year's growth, so a trimmed hedge, rather than one cut back to the trunk, bears fruit buried well within the hedge itself. A weary fieldfare or redwing, fresh in from Russia on migration, recovers from its hard journey by gobbling the rich diet provided in the hedge. But if the feast is borne on the outer reaches of the hedge, the traveller easily becomes sparrowhawk food or simple pickings for buzzards, kites or deep-diving peregrines. Far better for these members of the thrush family to fill their crops in the heart of the hedgerow, where thorn and barb protect them from curved beak and raking talon. A hedgerow management plan's sole purpose is to create a mosaic of hedgerows across farms with hedges at different points of management and care. Incorporating the flail into these plans, and working with the operators, making them as much a part of the management process as the planter, hedgelayer or coppicer, reconnects farm workers with hedgerows. This notion may sound on the surface like some New Age hokum, yet hedges are very much a human endeavour, and if we are going to see a return of healthy hedgerows on farms, we must regain the lost human connection with them.

Of course the flail can be, and is, abused. Lazy operators, ill-trained operators or simply the student operator bored now the excitement of harvest is over, can all smash a hedge rather than trim it. The flail is a machine capable of destruction, and in heavy hands it is no conservationist's tool at all. A hedge can be butchered to a pile of flayed sticks in a mere handful of passes. Bizarrely, this destructive power is aided and abetted by a government grant. The BE3 grant was a Defra quick-fix notion, created to appease both the farmers who wanted a form of payment to cut their hedges and the ecologists who wanted farmers to encourage taller, wider hedges. The grant pays £10 per hundred metres for one side of a hedge to be left uncut for three years. This compromise was and remains, like many such compromises that try to please all parties, a near-abject failure. Hedges managed under the BE3 become lopsided, shading out one side whilst the other becomes bashed and broken, due to the flail having to churn through growth that is far too thick for the machine to cut effectively. Thankfully the new SFI hedgerow standard encourages a system of incremental cutting. This pragmatic and practical solution pays farmers to incrementally allow their hedges to become wider and taller, by cutting ten centimetres or so above the knuckle left from the previous cut. The flail of course is perfect for this role, making a neat job of the fine brash, turning the cut material into beneficial fibrous mulch which is returned to the hedge base. The fruit is retained and the hedge is shaped to maximise the surface area, thereby augmenting the hedgerow as a habitat feature.

Michael Dixon drove the tractor and flail at Quenby. To my way of thinking, if such a sage, pragmatic and caring soul as he was satisfied with the tool as an overall good thing for hedgerows, then that should be all the recommendation any of us needs.

9

Enemies?

I have no need for an alarm to wake me; there are rooks in the oaks at the end of my garden. Starting in early February, when they first begin crafting their treetop nurseries, an ongoing, and entirely one-sided, neighbourly dispute kicks off between them and me. Through my bedroom window, ajar regardless of season, I hear their background guttural bubbling begin long before the dawn breaks. The rooks lend their voice to a choir of countless other birds. There are thrushes and blackbirds, robins, wrens, a carrion and a pheasant. Wheezing tits and whirring finches, chack-chacking jackdaws . . . and there are pigeons too, all singing in praise of the dawn light that appears in the east. The rookery bubble becomes a babble as the warming orb feels its way up through strips of cloud and they turn to it and bow, a sun seemingly held aloft by the limbs of the crack willows that fringe the water meadows beyond my garden hedge.

All the fifteen or so couples who live in the rookery are unabashed thieves. True couples they are too; rooks mate for life – although, in the event of a death, the widow or widower's mourning period is brief. I watch the rooks when I first venture out of the back door to sniff the air. I see them silhouetted against a new sky as they pilfer goods and chattels from their neighbours. Should one get caught in the act by a fellow householder, an altercation ensues. There are screams, stabbing beaks and black-wing waving, a war of words waged far above me in the swaying tops.

There seems no obvious benchmark for what, to rook eyes, constitutes an item of desirable building material. One sprig of nondescript smoky ash seems considered so wholly perfect by all present that it becomes a catalyst for battle. Another seemingly identical twig is disdainfully discarded, ignored and spat out to fall with a crack on the roof of my truck parked below. They also lob out stones, acorns and leaves, and seemingly endless streams of chalky shit that then decorates my windscreen, door handles and bonnet. Whenever I appear through the garden gate, the – for now – childless pairs call a brief ceasefire on their own squabbles to embark on a phalanx of caterwauling bellows by which they emphasise their disgust at my presence. I am in no way singled out for all this spite, however. Anyone or anything that dares to trespass within the unilaterally declared twenty-metre exclusion zone around the oaks which form the pillars of their commune is liable for abuse.

Nests are completed by March, added to and fiddled with in obsessive compulsion. Around this time a watchful cessation in hostilities is declared by the rookery residents. This doesn't include my dogs; they continue to receive their daily corvid hate – wolves will always be wolves to birds, even if we think we made them into spaniels. Each hen rook lays four to five speckled larimar-hued eggs. The cocks are attentive, and brooding is shared between sexes. While one fluffs breast feathers over eggs, the other goes off foraging for beetles, worms, acorns, berries and dunnock chicks. It's a varied diet in the rookery. Whenever a partner returns, a chattering yodel erupts from the sitting tenant, spreading like Chinese whispers among the other residents of the twiggy terraces: the volume seems to reflect the quality of the offering. Through binoculars I once saw one returning spouse bear an entire pat of butter. Who knows where this bounty, clutched in a muddy beak, was pilfered from. It was clearly an item of great envy within the community and I saw the butter-thief's eyes glitter with seeming pride, bringing sparkling life to the ghost-grey featherless face.

My rook neighbours are at their quietest in early summer, being fully preoccupied with the task of turning fluffy, milky hatchlings into glossy, ebonised juveniles. Barren eggs, lifeless carcasses, weakling chicks and yet more shit are all ejected from the now-teetering stacks of homely sticks to land on my unfortunate truck. Each day I find a sorry spread of nature's detritus strewn across the bonnet or the shingle of my weed-filled drive. After hatching, the rookery chorus becomes sing-song, sounding to my ears like a lullaby. By May the 'branchers', as the fledged yet flightless youngsters are known, make their staggering way, sidling crabwise along the oaken limbs, halting at the bowing tips, where they then spread weakling wings. Facing beaks to the wind, the chattering youth flap and flex in rigorous bouts of callisthenics, building muscles, stretching tendons, first feeling then mastering the effect of wind upon remiges. Their parents drift watchfully on thermals overhead, then with wings tucked they dive, applying brakes to swoop over their offspring, enticingly cackle-calling, telling them, I guess, about what it means to fly. Finally, one accepts the challenge, claws loosen their grip on a branch and then one after another, young rooks take a gamble and tumble up to become dark marks in the East Anglian air.

The clamouring and cawing and squeals dwindle in my ears as bird after young bird follows its parents and embraces the clouds. To me, their behaviour appears clearly to be, as we humans understand it, joy. Joy at being airborne, joy at being freed from that world of twigs, shit and detritus. A few, either too precocious or too weak, are the losers. Failing to soar, they fall like sycamore keys, spiralling to the ground in a soft crumple. If they survive, they panic on the green below. With a prancing gait they bound about, staring up, making plaintive pleas for parental protection, demanding food and help, a return to the safety of the treetops, none of which ever comes. Occasionally one may be fortunate, and with much flapping, catches a scant thermal finding a branch or the roof of my house. They cling there to draw breath, panting with a blinking expression of the trauma they have just experienced. There they wait for many minutes, summoning energy and courage, before trying once again to join their extended family wheeling up high. Most fail and are killed by hawks or cats or crows. Sometimes they survive the day, but the cold, hunger or foxes and badgers of night will claim them after the sun sets. My son used to try to help these pathetic failures; they sulked and then died. Unlike a magpie, crow or raven, rooks revile domesticity.

By autumn the rooks have long forgotten eggs, and brooding and fledging and first flight. The commune remains, but only tight-knit at roosting, for the whole living quietly; this is a peaceful time for them in their waving oak tops. They feed in the plough and wade through the drills; when perched they wait for gales to blow so they may indulge in aerobatics and shout profanities at the wind. When February returns, they will treat me once more like an unwelcome interloper. I have no need to watch TV soap operas when there are rooks in the oaks at the end of my garden.

I SEE MORE OF rooks than I do my wife and son. They wake me with shouts outside my window at dawn, then, through my rear-view mirror, I see them wave a garrulous goodbye as I trundle my truck in lurches over the potholes of my crumbling drive. When I arrive at whichever farm hedge I am laying, it is invariably rook voices that provide the overall soundtrack for the day, as they feed in fields or watch our thorny toil from some viewpoint in the tops of nearby woods. When I turn my vehicle back up the drive, I hear my dogs in the back sing in discordant delight at being home from work; the rooks in their oak tops ruffle mantles in a muttering and reluctant good evening, silhouetted in the last light of day.

Most days rooks are the farmer's friend, gorging their crops to bursting on agricultural pests – slugs, leatherjackets, wireworms, cockchafer grubs – these and countless other invertebrates of the topsoil are studiously snaffled. Observing a rook's beak, you see clearly that this is largely an honest tool, an artisan's device, completely unlike the glittering assassin's dagger sported by its close cousin the carrion crow. The rook's maw is designed for digging. The skin behind that shovel is naked and tough – woodsmoke grey as far as the eye – evolved, I suppose, to prevent plumage from being fouled as they delve. Yet only a fool would believe the rook is wholly John Barleycorn; he turns quite readily into a foe when the seasons and weather change. Rooks then gaggle to follow the lines of a seed drill. Teams of them track the rows with a stiff, wide-legged gait, like that of a politician who forgets to bring his wellies to a farm visit. They chuckle and mew conversationally to one another, picking their methodical way through beans, peas or seed corn, preferably just as they germinate and provide a delicious combination of sweet sugars and protein. The rook, along with his corvid cousins, the carrion crow, the jackdaw and the magpie, are all species named on GL42, one of the three general licences for bird control, which permits a landowner to kill these named species in order to prevent crop damage or the spread of disease.

In July, when the sun bakes the soils to a summer crisp, the rook's beak turns from muddy to bloody. No longer able to find sustenance in the ground, its attentions turn to the birds, mammals and invertebrates of the hedge and margin. Once more in regimental fashion the black squads march, this time among the tussocks, snapping a beetle here, a grey-partridge egg there, a juvenile vole here, a fledgling linnet there. Curiously, whilst crows and magpies are included on the general licence (GL40) that permits lethal control in order to conserve endangered birds, the rook gets a free pass and is therefore protected. Should a land manager seek to protect their grey partridges, yellowhammers and so on from the attention of the rook, he must apply to Defra for a specific licence, but before this licence is granted it must first be proved that red-listed species are in fact being killed – a clear case of closing the stable door long after the horse has bolted.

The Great War poet Charles Hamilton Sorley knew the rooks' carnivorous bent all too well. Although a Scot, Sorley was commissioned into the Suffolk Regiment. The Cambridge graduate was in the same battalion as my maternal grandfather, who thought Cambridge was a foreign place. Both fought in the bloody, muddy mess that was Loos. Grandad Roly sustained wounds there that scarred him for life. Sorley lost his, felled by a sniper near Hulluch. In his poem 'Rooks', Sorley writes: 'There, where the rusty iron lies, / The rooks are cawing all the day. / Perhaps no man, until he dies, / Will understand them, what they say.' At first glance it appears Sorley, as a subaltern in this Flanders charnel house, had a notably less cordial relationship with rooks than I do. To me rooks are largely comedic, only occasional pests, thieving beans and slaying chicks. To Sorley they are spectres, feasting on flesh – his comrades, and strung out like mole carcasses on a gibbet of barbed wire. Yet, reading the poem again, I glean that, like me, the poet cannot wholly revile the rook. The Suffolk Scot understood that it was he and his men, and the Germans on the other side of no man's land, who had foisted themselves upon the birds, bringing human war into an avian world. The trenches are temporary; the rookery is permanent, the residents of which have learned and will continue to learn our human ways, turning us to their advantage wherever possible. Be it in farming or in war, the rook comes out the winner. Who can hate a rook for simply being a rook?

Yet I have no qualms over killing rooks when the seeds sprout or the grey partridges lay their eggs. I view their lethal control in the same light as I do the culling of foxes who take grey-partridge broods, or of non-native deer whose gross populations decimate hedgerow and woodland habitats. There is a balance to be maintained, and with humans being the only top predator left standing, the job falls to us. The BTO estimates there are 1.4 million rooks in Britain, while the number of grey partridge pairs is thought to be around 40,000. It seems to me nonsensical to spend my year improving habitats and providing plentiful food sources to support this red-listed farmland bird and then watch idly as eggs and chicks are snaffled up by the beak of a rook. The three-legged stool, of food, habitat, and predator control, is to my mind the epitome of nature – balanced, honest and cruel.

I like birds. Which, I suppose, is an essential state of mind for a hedgelayer. Countless bird species, along with my on/off pals the rooks, are a daily companion. Birds seem so willing to share their home with me, it is as if they twig, despite all of the noise I make with a chainsaw or my seemingly brutal actions with a billhook, that I am on their side. In bouts of anthropomorphic reverie, I feel part of an exclusive club, of which only feathered folk and me are members. I know there are countless invertebrates, amphibians and small mammals that benefit from my work too, but they rarely stop to see what I am up to. When a wood mouse catches sight of me, he has fear in his eye; a titmouse,* meanwhile, looks on with the appearance of genuine curiosity. The hedge plays home to vast swathes of wildlife, so working within it becomes a job of complete immersion in nature. Hedgelaying for me has two chief drivers. First, and

---

* Old country name for a blue tit.

most importantly, hedgelaying pays my bills. I reckon that in a good season I can earn a sniff more than an Ipswich bus driver. That is, of course, wholly dependent upon the weather – snow or heavy rain stops play. Second, all the scratches on my arms, the plucks and bleeding tears across my face, the perpetual ringing in my ears from the chainsaw's roar, the back pain, the windburn, the cold feet, and the red-rimmed eyes from spitting bar oil is all, more or less, worth it, because my job is so obviously beneficial to wildlife. Yet if I am honest, it is largely for the birds. Birds and hedgerows go together. The hedge is the very stuff of life for so many of the avian species who call East Anglian farmland home. Yet in nature one size, or hedge, doesn't fit all.

If every hedgerow on the farm was laid, then trimmed and maintained so as to be a perfect height for linnet, yellowhammer, dunnock and grey partridge, the result would be little better than having no hedges at all. One of the chief reasons for undertaking hedgerow management plans in the first place is to prevent a hedgerow monoculture occurring, instead ensuring a 'mosaic' is formed, then maintained. This mosaic is created in a roughly twenty-year cycle of management; naturally, soil variations and localised climate make this a rule of thumb rather than one set in stone. The cycle starts with major intervention – either a new hedge planted, an existing sparse-based or gappy one laid, or an overgrown monster coppiced. The next stage is that of ongoing management. Once the hedgerow has begun its regrowth it is cut, trimmed and shaped, allowed to grow and tiller out, becoming incrementally taller and wider and, most importantly, thicker from base to tip. However hard we may try in the management phase, growth will always win out in the end; the cycle turns and, after a few decades, the hedge requires major intervention once more and out comes the billhook, chainsaw or tree shear. By ensuring that every hedge on a farm is at various stages of this management cycle, it is possible to maximise the number and range of habitats demanded by numerous bird species.

The low, tightly interwoven nature of a recently laid hedge does just fine for grey partridge. For them a hedge has two fundamental roles, first as a windbreak, and more vitally as an air raid shelter under which they find security from raptor attack overhead. For the grey, the tussock grasses that proliferate in the hedgerow's lee are their preferred nesting ground, and source of food both in the form of seeds and greenstuff for adults and squishy insects for chicks. A grey partridge would never lower itself to perch up in a hedge, or a pear tree for that matter.

While the yellowhammer does use the topmost tips of a hedge for display, it nests low down in the hedgerow base. For these gaudy little mixtures of mustard and *café au lait*, a combination of grass margin lined by tight-knit hedgerows – preferably lower than three metres – with blocks of seed or arable stubble beyond is just about as good as it gets. Now that the yellowhammer is red-listed, its presence, like that of the grey partridge, is a barometer for the efficacy of lowland farmland conservation. While many humans claim they 'hate the flail', the yellowhammer delights in its aftermath, relishing the densely crowded lattice of branches created by the passing of the blades. With the removal of cattle from most East Anglian agricultural rotations now – environmentalists hate cow burps, and supermarkets hate to pay the price for slow-grown British grass-fed beef – very few hedgerows today are kept tight through bovine power. Instead, regular trimming interventions by a tractor-mounted flail or cutter are the only option for creating and maintaining the multi-frond mesh of impenetrable thorn so essential for yellowhammer breeding success. Nest building begins in early April, with the passerines crafting a tightly woven nursery of dead grass fronds glued together by mud and spittle, safely tucked close to the ground; within this stockade of spike, brooding can take place largely hidden from corvid eye and raptor talon.

Linnets and redpolls share similar nesting tastes to the yellowhammers. For them, the presence of some prickling briar in the hedge seems to be a boon, yet for the hedge itself bramble is largely a negative. Bramble is a precocious plant, growing with a vigour that leads to its becoming an invasive strangler, killing off the slower-growing true shrubby hedgerow species. In our hedgerow management rotations, we invariably advocate coppicing hedgerow bramble to the ground – it will come back anyway – and recommend instead that farmers leave field corners to become rougher and wilder. Here the bramble can find a place where it is of maximum benefit to wildlife and of little if any hindrance to agriculture or the hedge itself. If that bramble-clump corner sports some blackthorn sucker and an ivy-clad dead elm or two, so much the better. Within these scrubby, brambly, unruly corners of mayhem the dunnock, or hedge sparrow, nests close to the ground. The hen dunnock is a promiscuous lady, undertaking multiple matings with numerous males, producing a nest filled with eggs of mixed DNA. It is not only a canny course of action, guaranteed to thicken up the gene pool, but also leads to every favoured male feeling duty bound to take on a parenting role, in an avian homage to *Trois hommes et un couffin*.

A hedge fit for a yellowhammer is a hateful place for a turtle dove to rear its family. These purring summer migrants from Africa choose a hedgerow that to most would seem to be no hedge at all, more a straggling line of trees. For them a lanky field maple, overgrown hawthorn, dead elm or pollarded ash is ideal; the hedge beneath, if worthy of the name, need be nothing more than a few clumps of failing thorn or hazel. Such habitats are becoming all too rare, many falling victim to landowners 'tidying things up'; more often than not, though, they are felled to make way for yet more village-edge property development. At the topmost branches of these barely-hedgerow trees, turtle doves build a nest of twigs so pathetic and tardy in construction that, in a strong breeze, their off-white eggs topple out and smash below. It is little wonder really that the turtle dove is scarce; modern life doesn't suit them. If they do survive their late-springtime migration from sub-Saharan Africa and make it to eastern and southern England, having run a gauntlet of hunters in southern Europe (although there is currently a well-observed moratorium on turtle dove hunting in Spain, Italy and France), they must then find a very specific and increasingly rare habitat to nest in. Being fussy feeders, their diet is solely that of small seeds; their preferred dining table is a short-clipped grass track, such as that found by a sheep-mown track or a topped ride as seen at Flea Barn. That being said, a concrete farmyard is acceptable. They equally require a plentiful source of accessible water to wash down this granivorous diet, such as a farm pond or gently banked slow-flowing stream. If all of the stars align and they do find this markedly specific combination of habitat and food, not to mention a partner, their measly nests, with little to no top cover, are readily predated by overly abundant magpies, carrion crows, rooks and jackdaws. The squabs meanwhile are particularly vulnerable to buzzards and kites and the diminutive adults are just as likely to be picked off by sprawk or peregrine. Every East Anglian countryman or -woman over the age of forty has the turtle dove's call etched deeply in their DNA; the rolling purr is, or at least was, a sound integral to a Suffolk high summer. The fact that the lazy, dreamy trill is now largely silenced is barely comprehensible to many, and much like the concerted and successful campaign to bring the Suffolk barn owl back from the brink, turtle dove conservation is being vigorously embraced by the county's farmers and naturalists.

Nightingales nest in scrub that is thick from bottom to top. The massive West Country hedgerows that I remember from my schooldays certainly held these crepuscular songsters, yet, here in the East, few such hedges exist, and it is the scruffy scrub blocks and 'scratty' woods that suit nightingales best. Cover-laying these small coverts, planted as pheasant cover (or as it was when the hounds still hunted foxes) helps their cause. But the muntjac undo much of our work, eating out the understorey in short order. Blackbirds require hedgerow trees, as do the song and mistle thrushes, making their nests where bough meets trunk. Great, blue, coal and long-tailed tits, too, adore a tree in a hedge, but they seek out the hollows and cavities created by old knot holes. We frequently leave some standing dead wood in our laid hedgerows, particularly those alongside woodland edges, knowing that in particular the willow tit looks for well-rotted material in which to excavate its burrow-like nest. The grey partridges, of course, would rather there were no hedgerow trees at all, either living or dead; they have evolved to know these are perches for enemies – buzzards, sprawks* and carrion crows in particular. You will rarely, if ever, find a grey partridge nesting anywhere near a tree in a hedge. For that matter, lapwings, skylarks and stone curlew not only hate trees, they despise hedgerows too. It is the wide-open spaces that suit them, for they, like the grey, know that death perches above and death's eye is clear and death's beak is hooked and its talons sharp. Evolution says to them, stay out in the open and trust in luck, remain motionless and develop artful camouflage to protect your eggs and young rather than relying on fronds of thorn and barb to guard them. Bullfinches can do without hedgerow trees, yet they need a hedge to nest in that is at least four metres tall, preferably as thick and prickly as the ones I knew well in Leicestershire. A chiffchaff needs none of that height; a coppiced hedge, with dead-hedging over the stools, is more than sufficient for their parenting needs. Garden warblers, too, like this sort of low-grown habitat. (Mind you, I see more garden warblers on farms than I do in gardens, most likely due to the pressures placed upon them by human disturbance and domestic cats.) The charity Songbirds UK claims there are nearly 11 million cats in

---

* Old country name for a sparrowhawk.

Great Britain. These domestic pets are, they say, responsible for killing some 55 million birds each year. Even if that figure is wayward by 50 per cent, it seems curious that the RSPB resists calling for any restrictions on cat ownership, or legislated preventative measures, to help reduce these unnecessary song and farmland bird deaths. The garden warbler is a dowdy little thing that belies its chortlingly joyous song of spring. I find the birds proliferate in recently laid farmland hedgerows, seeming to choose a spot with a ditch on the southern side. Whitethroats want a hedge akin to Goldilocks's porridge – not too tall, not too short, just right; if there is a line of trees immediately behind the hedge, that's better still for these diminutive snowy-bibbed birds.

This brief snapshot of the gross variation required in nesting-habitat requirements highlights the pressing need for what to some may seem the overly intricate and methodical management-planning that Gouldy and I advocate. It is clear the reasons for the almost free-fall decline in many of our farmland bird species are multi-faceted, yet habitat loss is undoubtedly one of the leading causes. Farmland habitat loss is frequently taken to mean the decline in the numbers of hedgerows since 1945, yet to my mind this is an all-too-simplistic view. To say 'we've lost half our hedgerows since the war' is, as we have already seen, largely hyperbole; we have never known precisely the quantity (or quality) of English hedgerows at any point in our history. What is a fact is that the hedge has always been in a state of fluctuating boom and bust, reflecting the relative prosperity of agriculture and changes in farming practice. Whilst it is truthful to say we have fewer hedges now than in 1939, this is not necessarily the primary cause of farmland bird decline. To my mind, the decimation of insects, caused by ongoing and historic pesticide use, has wreaked far more long-term biodiversity damage than any grubbed-out hedge has done. But, in habitat terms, the loss of hedges post 1945 is not the prescient issue; it is the decline in rotational management, and therefore the loss of hedgerow mosaics.

Hedges only truly maximise their benefit to wildlife, particularly birdlife, if they are in a mosaic state. This condition can only be created through rotational management that relies upon time-consuming, high-cost and labour-heavy traditional methods, such as laying and coppicing, followed by ongoing incremental trimming using flails or cutters. Thanks to the now financially imperative dominance of mechanisation in farming, particularly in arable systems, our hedgerow network has ultimately suffered. The old lines of rotationally hand-managed hedgerows, with their varying widths and heights, have largely gone or at least have morphed, replaced by a monotone, machine-cut sameness. The simple narrative expounded by many groups and individuals that nature has declined because we have lost 50 per cent or more of our hedges since 1945 avoids, by a country mile, the most important point. The true missing element for English farmland hedgerows today is the expert human resource on farms to manage them properly. What is abundantly clear is that the clamour to plant more hedges will only compound this situation. Yes, we may physically have more hedgerows, but without any planning as to how these hedges will be managed, and by whom, all we will have done is increase a shrub monoculture, which may keep the carbon obsessives happy, but will do little to reverse biodiversity decline.

My passion for birds is heartfelt yet somewhat generalist. Gouldy's bird lore is fairly exclusive, some may say obsessive. He places grey partridges above any other species, knowing nearly all there is to know of their needs and wants; to him the grey is more than a mere bird. It was, and in many ways still is, his life. Yet if we are to achieve a truly meaningful mosaic of hedgerows, managed in such a way as to provide sustainable habitat and food sources for the entire gamut of threatened farmland bird species, one needs not only willing landowners, and skilled practical hedgerow managers to carry out the donkey work; it is also essential to gain the advice, input and expertise of true ornithologists. I am fortunate to work with two exceptional examples of this tribe.

Mark Nowers and Eliza Leat work for the RSPB as conservation officers for Operation Turtle Dove in Essex and Suffolk. Their role is dedicated to halting and reversing species decline, chiefly by advising and supporting farmers to create and better manage habitats and provide turtle-dove-specific supplementary food. I have worked with the pair on and off for over three years. I would count both as friends as well as colleagues. This programme is a fine example of all that is best about the RSPB, using its remarkable connections internationally, from government level all the way down to local farmers across the turtle dove's flyway. The goodwill I see for the project here in East Anglia is down to two factors. First, the turtle dove itself, a charismatic little bird whose decline has been so sudden, yet the reversal of which seems so tangible. Second, it is down to people, namely Mark and Eliza; the pair are likeable, they listen and inform rather than preach or judge, all traits highly regarded among rural communities. I cannot think of one farmer who, after meeting one or both of these conservationists, hasn't felt inspired to do their bit for the threatened dove, by beginning supplementary feeding, creating feed rides, undertaking corvid control and managing habitat. Yet the RSPB itself is much like the rook, receiving a mixed reception from the agricultural community, sometimes seen as friend and sometimes foe. This state of affairs seemingly has nothing to do with the likes of Eliza or Mark, but everything to do with the charity's communication and policies teams.

The RSPB dubs itself 'Nature's Voice'. This voice has become increasingly combative, particularly towards agriculture and game-shooting interests, so much so that the NFU has described a series of the charity's public campaigns as 'shameful', 'unhelpful' and 'anti-farming'. It could be argued the war of words between farming and the RSPB truly started bubbling in 2011, when the charity's outgoing head of conservation Dr Mark Avery took a hefty swing in a *Guardian* article, stating that 'they [farmers] are fundamentally anti-environment', adding,

'The NFU lacks a coherent view of what the future of farming should look like except that the cheques must keep coming from the taxpayer.' Dr Avery is a mercurial character, unashamedly blunt with a seeming inbuilt dislike for working-class people in tweed, although toffs wearing the same receive an easier ride. Yet for all that, I have a sneaking regard for him; he is clearly a knowledgeable naturalist and when not playing up to the crowd, as I think he was in his 2011 statement, he seems at heart a pragmatist. Since then, the public rift between the RSPB executive and British farming has visibly grown wider. Numerous critical social media posts and newspaper editorials, originating either directly from the RSPB communications department or their portfolio of celebrity ambassadors, has helped to create an acrimonious relationship between the charity and its supporters on the one hand and the NFU, farmers and land managers on the other. Most recently the charity's senior policy officer Phil Carson claimed in a blog post for the RSPB website that due to the cessation of EU cross-compliance regulations, farmers would now be free to damage hedgerows and use chemicals on margins 'to maximise short-term economic gains'. Not only is this factually incorrect, inasmuch as hedgerows continued to be highly protected under the Wildlife and Countryside Act; it was also a clearly confrontational statement made seemingly to incite a backlash from the NFU and their members – proving little has changed at head office since 2011 when it comes to the RSPB's views on farmers. Conspicuously, when the new post-Brexit legislation on cross-compliance was announced in early 2024, it became clear to all that these new protections were in fact even stronger than those previously enshrined under the EU law. Sadly, the RSPB remained notably quiet, neither admitting Carson's 'mistake' nor praising what, to many people's surprise, including my own, was a political decision with practical wildlife conservation at its core. Even the Conservative party itself has become a target for attack by the RSPB. In September

2023, the official RSPB Twitter account posted a tweet (which was later deleted) stating Rishi Sunak, Michael Gove and Thérèse Coffey were 'liars', listing a series of environmental commitments that the charity claimed the then Tory government had been guilty of reneging on. As a result of this spat, Beccy Speight, the RSPB chief executive, was forced after pressure from the Charities Commission to make a fulsome apology and an embarrassing climb-down. It later became apparent that whilst Beccy took the public rap, the tweet had in fact been made unilaterally by her communications team without her prior knowledge or sanction. I met Beccy in 2021 when she visited Flea Barn, invited to see for herself the positive impacts for farmland birds that Ed Nesling's model of combining sustainable farming, game shooting and three-legged-stool conservation made. I found her approachable and professional, if obviously not actually that much at home on a farm – those pesky binoculars slung low always give people away! I took the opportunity to ask her if the RSPB's tone and language, particularly that used by her patrons, hampered a 'middle ground' of consensus being found between her organisation and those in the agricultural and practical conservation communities. I cited, amongst others, a statement by RSPB president Dr Amir Khan, who tweeted the following in October 2022: 'Shooting birds for pleasure doesn't make you more of a man/woman/person but it does make you less of a human being.' Beccy countered by saying, 'I can't tell [him] what to say, patrons are volunteers'. I bumped into the then Defra secretary of state Thérèse Coffey a few days later at a farming event and asked for her feelings on being called a thrice-liar by the RSPB; she replied, 'That won't be forgotten or forgiven.'

This war of words between the RSPB, farmer types, shooting types and Tory types may seem nothing more than a puffing display of posturing, politicking and peddling, but this turf war has become yet another obstacle and hindrance to the recovery of farmland bird species. Sixty-nine per cent of England's land mass is farmland. In Mid Suffolk that figure is 97 per cent. This land, although on the whole currently intensively farmed, is, or certainly should be, the place where biodiversity decline is halted. Agriculture has its faults, no doubt. Some flaws are of its own making; most, however, are instigated by the demands of the market. Likewise, there are some shoots and gamekeepers who are criminals, polluting woodlands through overstocking game birds and illegally killing protected species. But to portray the actions of wrongdoing individual farmers, gamekeepers and landowners as representative of the whole is the worst of straw-man arguments. Creating the 'Us v Them' narrative seems to help the RSPB in its funding campaigns: they have been remarkably adept in garnering donations and maintaining their profile in both mainstream and social media as the nation's best-known wildlife charity. The RSPB's income rose from £147 million in 2019 to over £150 million in 2022, of which £126 million came from the general public in donations and legacies. The confrontational social media usage doubtless also helps boost the profiles and egos of some C-list celebrities. Yet such behaviour does nothing positive for wildlife. Alienating the very people who hold the keys to the land where wildlife lives, rather than partnering with them in the tumultuous post-Brexit period of agricultural transition, is just as damaging for farmland biodiversity as flailing a hedge to bits or spraying a water course with fungicide. However, while the RSPB and NFU wrestle, the Countryside Alliance and Chris Packham butt horns, and BASC and Wild Justice wave their metaphorical willies at one another, out in the fields a different tune is being played.

My own experience of working with the RSPB at the coal face of conservation is nothing but positive. The confrontational, anti-farming, anti-game-shooting, overtly political rhetoric that I read and hear from head office is absent in the trenches. Mark and Eliza show a clear level of understanding of the financial constraints farmers currently face and the impacts this has on wildlife and rural communities. I have never heard this pair judge and damn farmers as being 'anti-nature' or a gamekeeper as 'less than human'. I first met them when they came to Flea Barn, Eliza to assess and advise on turtle dove conservation, Mark to map the wider avian health of the farm. The depth of knowledge Mark has of bird identification, habits, habitat and song is remarkable. A hedgerow wander with him is much like one with Gouldy: he sees what to most is unseen and hears where most are deaf. Since Ed adopted the three-legged-stool approach to managing his hedges, edges, wetlands and woods, the increase in yellowhammer, greenfinch, goldfinch and linnet was obvious. The question we had was precisely by how many had the numbers increased, and more importantly where were the numbers increasing most readily and why. Mark and Eliza helped provide the answers.

In the modern agricultural landscape, bird surveys, indeed any study of the soil, flora and fauna, are becoming increasingly important. One of the most profitable crops now being produced in modern agriculture is not cereal, dairy or meat, but data. Data, or the verifiable figures that a farmer can collate of his or her farm's biodiversity net gain, of the carbon captured and stored, of energy efficiencies made, and of the wider environmental benefits provided for society, now all have a financial value. Currently the precise cash value of much of this data is largely unknown, or at best guessed at. Carbon traders abound, talking in numbers and using terminology that is guaranteed to either scare or snare the unwary. If a farm can first be made carbon neutral through more sustainable production methods, sowing permanent leys, creating woodland, or planting and managing hedgerows, any additional carbon the land then sequesters and stores can be sold to third parties, invariably a deal organised by traders. While some of these traders are honest brokers, some seem more reminiscent of *Dad's Army*'s Private Walker flogging pilfered fuel to Corporal Jones. There are growing questions over who these businesses are that the traders are dealing with. More than 75 per cent of the leading enterprises now buying carbon credits on the global market are themselves either fossil-fuel companies or car manufacturers. They are able to claim every tonne of carbon credit they purchase from a British farmer as their own, meaning as long as they pay others to do the clean work, they can continue doing the dirty stuff. This may indicate why Shell – the largest buyer of carbon credits in the world – can still confidently claim, on paper, it is ahead of schedule to achieve net zero by 2050. In 2023 the Advertising Standards Authority banned a number of Shell's TV and YouTube ads, finding they misled the public on the climate and environmental benefits of the group's products overall.

'Biodiversity offsetting' remains an equally grey area, with the promise of big bucks for farmers who increase the environmental 'public good' of their land. As yet there is no precise calibration for what a landowner will be paid by a property developer, supermarket or banker for habitats created or species returned. Yet at least you can physically see a well-laid hedge, a lapwing flock or the bobbing heads of wildflowers in a reconstructed meadow rather than the invisibility of carbon. Businesses, particularly those in the chemical, food manufacturing, construction and finance sectors, are all too aware that their practices are either directly or indirectly responsible for pollution and the destruction of habitats and species. Farmers, by adopting nature-friendly methods of crop and livestock production, can offset these losses and make the nature denuders pay for the privilege. Likewise, landowners are financially recompensed by utility companies for ensuring water is cleaner, energy is greener and air purer. It is a challenge for many old-school farmers to comprehend that their job today is no longer solely growing food. Yet the direction of travel is evident. James Black, one of the most experienced and highly regarded commercial arable and pig farmers in East Anglia, noted at the Suffolk Farming Conference in 2020, 'We must embrace the idea that our land is no longer solely there to produce food. Our job is now to grow fuel. We will store carbon for others, we will farm wildlife for all.'

Collecting and collating all of this environmental data, which may well be of significant financial value in the future, is, however, a challenging harvest to reap. True experts, like Mark and Eliza, are no mere ornithologists and naturalists; they are the contract harvesters of a valuable crop called data.

It would be no exaggeration to say that Mark and Eliza have been instrumental in changing and moulding my current thinking on farmland bird conservation. They have taught me to look more holistically at how hedgerows connect and link habitats together. I think I first coined the term 'creating a mosaic of hedgerows' when walking around Flea Barn's margins with Mark as he carried out a bird-nesting habitat survey. I grow increasingly incredulous that these two thoroughly good, practical and pragmatic people are part of the same organisation that seems so hell-bent on enlarging the gulf between farming/shooting communities and the wider environmental lobby. The same positivity can be extended to the remarkable young team I met who run the RSPB's Hope Farm. I visited the charity's demonstration farm to take a look at their hedgerows in the company of a number of local farmers. From the outset I felt a sense of joint endeavour between the Hope Farm team and their guests. Everyone present was trying to find the best means of farming profitably and sustainably with nature without negatively impacting the wider environment. Our challenges, I discovered, were theirs too. I also learned more about English elm trees in one afternoon than I have in a lifetime of living and working around the poor old things! Ultimately, I gleaned that we are the same; we just wore different badges on our hats, mine a GWCT grey partridge, theirs the RSPB avocet. Why, I wondered when I drove back from Hope Farm, does it all go so wrong away from the coal face? Why has the RSPB's public relationship with farming and shooting become so acrimonious? Chasing money, a clamour for attention and social media: these things seem to ruin most things in life, I concluded.

10

Regrowth

I wait under the spread fingers of a sweet chestnut. Its leaves cast their rippling pattern on the sandy ground. The branches overhead are sent bowing and waving by intermittent puffs of chill late-April breeze. I shuffle my feet with impatience, kicking up grit and spiny chestnut husks. Laid hedges, each only twenty metres in length, surround me on three sides like a letter U. The short length of hawthorn and hazel on my right was laid this time last year. The binders, now dried and cracked, remain twisted in place. New buds have erupted along the laid pleacher; from the heels spring upward shoots of precocious coppice growth. I think to myself, it's not a bad job on such a poor hedge.

At the dot of nine o'clock I see the first group of children make their way towards me. They remind me of a litter of foxhound puppies, all babbling, pushing and shoving one another, rough, but with no evil intent. Their teacher claps her hands and the racket ends abruptly. She turns and treats me to a smile of genuine pleasure. We recognise one another, meeting on this day each year for the past four. The Suffolk Schools Farm and Country Fair at Trinity Park is an institution well loved by teachers, children and exhibitors alike. Over one hundred Suffolk primary schools send their pupils to this event organised and run by the Suffolk Agricultural Association. Here they hear about food, farming and the countryside from the mouths of farmers, deer stalkers, beekeepers, naturalists and a solitary hedgelayer. This is the first stand of the day for the jolly teacher and her class of eight- and nine-year-olds. By two o'clock I know her smile will be well worn; herding cats is tiring, even for experienced hands like hers.

'Good morning, everyone,' I say to the upturned semi-circle of faces. 'My name is Richard. I'm a hedgelayer. Where are you from?' Twelve voices reply in a jumbled high-pitched chant. I only catch the last word – 'school'. I turn to the teacher, who smiles again and says 'Woodbridge'. I wave at the hedge on my left. 'What's this then?' I ask the children generally. Eleven hands immediately shoot skywards. One stays lowered; the twelfth child is distracted – he's watching a gundog-training demonstration in the distance; Labradors jumping gates are understandably more entertaining than hedges and pleachers. I point at a little girl, hair coiled in elaborate plaits, for her answer. I see she wears a replica Ipswich Town FC shirt; this is promotion year for The Tractor Boys, and their fan base is widening. Her blue wellies, decorated with green frogs holding brollies, make me smile – she has wedged them on the wrong feet. 'A bush?' she replies. 'Not quite,' I say. 'Trees?' answers a little boy sporting an Ipswich Town tracksuit. 'No, not trees.' 'Leaves?' says another; he goes against the grain hereabouts and wears a black beanie hat with an Arsenal badge. 'No, not quite!' The gundog fan turns around. 'A hedge,' he states matter-of-factly. I note his sweatshirt sports a John Deere tractor emblazoned on the midriff. 'Ye-e-s!' I enthuse, punching my right fist into my left palm. My exuberance spooks the audience, and the front row steps back half a stride. They bump into the rank behind, surprised that this odd, tall man in overalls is so excited about a mundane leafy line of things that look like small trees. I persevere, telling them why we have hedges on farms, how we manage them, what benefits they bring for wildlife, and how they ensure we have healthy food on our plates. I ask them what mammals they think live in a hedge. Their replies are eclectic. Some are obvious – mice, rabbits and snakes. Others leave me bemused. 'Cats?' says one little girl at the back. 'I have a cat called Ruby,' she adds confidentially, as if imparting scandalous gossip. 'One is a spiky little animal,' I add as a clue. John Deere finally gives me the answer I seek. 'Hedgehogs,' he announces. 'Ye-e-s.' I warm to my subject. 'Even their name reveals their preferred home, doesn't it?'

'Why would a thick, dense hedge be better for hedgehogs?' I ask. My audience pauses briefly, then, like Roman senators, all raise their hands. 'They don't like the rain?' says one boy, his Ipswich Town baseball cap too large for his head. 'They eat blackberries?' another little girl answers – her clothes revealing allegiance to neither football club nor tractor manufacturer; she prefers Taylor Swift. 'What if a hedge provides protection from being eaten? What might like to eat a hedgehog?' I query. This draws the gang up short. It is apparent they can't imagine anything wanting to crunch through all of those sharp spines, and anyway, in their gentle world of animal stories, the hedgehogs are little friends to all. They have yet to learn that true nature is far removed from the thing they read about in books; real nature is a series of terrifying episodes of eating or being eaten. I help the kids to find the right answer to the hedgehog's foe. 'It's black and white,' I add. The hands go up. 'Zebra?' says one. 'Skunk?' says another. 'No, not a skunk or a zebra – they don't live in Britain.' I begin to plead: 'What else is black and white and is a predator?' willing the right answer out of the class. Finally, the smallest boy in the front row raises his hand half-heartedly, a motion that could be passed off as an adjustment to his hair. 'Is it a badger?' he quavers. 'Ye-e-s!' I say. 'Badgers eat hedgehogs, and the thicker the hedge, the more chance a hedgehog has of escaping.'

I realise my question-and-answer session wasn't as fascinating for the children as it was enlightening for me. I grab my planting spade and a hawthorn whip. 'Right, who wants to help me plant a hedge and give the hedgehogs a new home?' I ask. Twelve hands shoot up and I give the spade to the little boy who knows what a badger is. Each child takes their turn at digging, planting, heeling and guarding, leaving a slightly crooked line of fledgling new hedge in their wake. 'I think that's a job well done, isn't it?' I say, and they agree wholeheartedly with a cheer. They say goodbye and wander off together, chattering and giggling. Their teacher turns and smiles a thank you over her shoulder, then, with arms outstretched, she shepherds her charges in the direction of a pig handling demonstration. The next class has arrived before my green cave. 'Good morning, everyone, my name is Richard, and I am a hedgelayer. Where are you from?'

IT IS NOT SO surprising that primary school children today know so little about the natural world around them. Some 80 per cent live in urban areas. The town- and cityscapes, which they have access to, have had much of the wild squeezed out of them. Public parks are sanitised and made safe. The canals and rivers nearby may be more akin to open sewers, littered and unwelcoming. Brownfield today is rarely a site of wilderness throwback, instead hidden and protected behind fencing and razor wire, viewed by the landowners as far too valuable to permit it to become an unofficial playground where kids can find grass snakes, slow worms or hedgehogs. Public transport is expensive, running restricted services at weekends and evenings; buses rarely venture out of the suburbs.

Even kids with more rural homes, such as those I met at Trinity Park, hailing from the small market town of Woodbridge, find the countryside an increasingly alien place. The free-range adventuring that I was permitted to indulge in as a child of the 1980s is vetoed by the majority of modern parents. Research by Save the Children in 2022 revealed a mere 27 per cent of British children aged between six and sixteen were permitted to play outside *at all* by their parents. The primary reason cited, with no little justification, was road safety. In the year of my birth, 13.5 million cars were on the road; today there are over 41 million. Even rural lanes run thick with traffic, making cycling and walking a hazardous pastime. Added to this were fears over children irritating their neighbours, or being told off by other users of open spaces. Parents have come to believe, if their offspring show an interest in wild things, that it is better they stay safe indoors and get their nature fix from the television or the internet.

For young people today, comprehension and appreciation of nature's rhythms are beginning to fade. This loss of understanding and inbuilt regard brings with it a devastating knock-on effect in later life, not only for the individual, but for wider society's relationship with nature, food and farming. If you don't know it, you won't love it, is the general idea. Our wildlife, our very land suffers as a result of this unintended ignorance. As the youngsters attending the Suffolk Schools Farming and Countryside Fair evidenced, there is a wholesale lack of understanding of something so commonplace as an English hedgerow, its plants and its denizens. Meanwhile, charismatic wildlife from continents far away are recognised and regarded. The conservationist Mary Colwell understood this looming tragedy all too well and doggedly campaigned for a new GCSE in natural history to become part of the National Curriculum. She succeeded – Mary is a remarkable campaigner, and it will be launched in 2025. Yet is beginning an education in nature at eleven already too late?

I think I was around eight years old when my parents gifted me a pair of hand-me-down binoculars; I passed them on to my own son thirty years later. They gave me my first dog at age ten. He became my primary excuse to leave the house at dawn and stay out until dusk. The poor little tyke, a terrier I named Skip, was of dubious pedigree and developed legs like a prize fighter from accompanying me on our long-distance natural adventures. My mother believes that she and my father avoided the standard conflicts seen between parents and pubescent children almost by accident. My mother is now in her late eighties, but remains as sharp as a tack. 'We bought you a dog, an air rifle and a bird book,' she told me over a cup of tea. 'We never saw you after that, you were always out watching things, messing about in hedges, trying to catch voles.' She then added, 'I got fed up with the smell of the rabbits you kept bringing home,' which came as a disappointment – I thought she appreciated my rabbiting skills. I now realise how lucky I am. The knowledge I gleaned about nature came to me via osmosis rather than via a screen; a fortunate child, growing up in the heart of a rural farming community.

Yet I was no loner, unlike the early conservationist John Muir, who spent days alone in nature, sleeping out under the stars, living off crusts of bread he carried in his pocket. He began rambling to escape his bullying father. I was luckier than Muir; my dad took me out in nature, encouraging in me a love for trees and the lines of shrubs we call hedgerows. He fascinated me by reeling off the old country names for the wildflowers; he taught me how they grow. I only remember him raising his voice to me twice – once when I was rude to the postman, and once for being too rough with one of our family dogs. I've been, largely, polite ever since and my house is forever filled with happy over-indulged dogs. My education in the land was not solely through my parents, however. Other self-appointed instructors inspired me too. Tony Butler, a gamekeeper, took me off feeding his pheasants at dawn and watching badgers in the gloom of dusk. In those moments of walking his woodland rides or waiting near a sett for brock to appear, he put the names to the birds whose songs we heard; he taught me how to shoot straight, graft an apple tree, train a dog and tame a ferret. Rose Whitcomb, the hobbling kennel-huntsman from the local pack of minkhounds, showed me how to identify one hedgerow nest from the next. She revealed to me the intricate life cycle of buzzards – or 'buzzwoods' as she insisted on calling them. She loved a buzzard as much as she did her shaggy hounds in their stinking yet scrupulously clean kennels. David Hopley, the local parson, drilled me in casting a fly and how to understand the life of rivers. It was through him I discovered that if you shut up, stand still and watch wildlife, you will witness dramas far more thrilling than any seen in a TV whodunnit. Then of course there was dear Michael Dixon. It was he who immersed me in hedges and grasslands; it is wholly thanks to him that I now view these agricultural features in terms of wildlife habitat and food provision. This all begs the question, why does this matter for hedgerows?

The hedge is a vital environmental and agricultural tool. Yet unlike most other agricultural devices, it requires more than practical know-how to maintain and keep working. The hedge demands a level of care, and – dare I say – love, without sounding like a wafty dreamer. Hedgelayers and coppicers I believe are made, not born. To be effective you have to simultaneously be an agriculturalist and a naturalist. I am repeatedly asked by people how I became a hedgelayer and I regale them with the tales of Michael and my time in the Leicestershire grass country. Yet, I realise, that while he taught me the mechanics, my other mentors completed the sum of the parts.

The Suffolk Agricultural Society understands that a holistic education in the countryside is essential. At their school fairs they show primary-school-aged children the entire gamut of today's working countryside. Alongside the tractors and combine harvesters sit beekeepers and hedgelayers; the pig farmers and agronomists have stands next to woodsmen, deer stalkers, ornithologists and entomologists. This not only opens the eyes of the youngsters to the variety of careers on offer within the rural economy, but demonstrates that each sector is largely and sometimes wholly reliant upon farming to keep the show on the road. If that link is made and a sufficient interest is awoken in young people, we have a chance of finding the next generation of hedgelayers.

Finding my replacement is important to me. I am now in my mid-fifties and each season the aches and pains of the job are felt that bit more keenly. How much longer I will continue laying hedges professionally is a topic of nearly daily debate with my wife, and my lumbar region. There are currently too few hedgelayers. There are six members of the National Hedge-laying Society working in the eastern region, twelve in the South East, a mere twenty in the East Midlands, the true heartland of hedging. That is not to say every working hedger is a member of the society – I'm not, for one; but even if the membership were doubled or tripled, it is clear there remains a shortage of hands. We now know there are approximately 390,000 kilometres of English hedgerows and that the government has drafted legislation to support planting an additional 72,500 kilometres of new whips. This adds up to over 460,000 kilometres of hedgerows, all of which will require laying or coppicing on a roughly twenty-year rotational cycle. This in turn means that we need at least 6,000 competent hedgers working in Britain in order to lay nearly 30,000 kilometres annually. Of course, each would need to maintain the pace that Gouldy and I do of laying around five kilometres each season to keep up!

There are some obvious answers – obvious to me, anyway – as to how to solve the national shortage of hedgers. First, we have the Young Farmers' Clubs (YFCs). There are 581 clubs nationally, with 28,000 members aged between ten and twenty-eight. The proportion of members who are sons or daughters in farming families reduces each year. Increasingly, Young Farmers are not actually farmers; they are instead a disparate group of young people who share an interest in agriculture, the countryside and rural life. I have recently taken four clubs from Suffolk and Norfolk on farm walks to show them the ecology of hedgerows and the practices employed in their management. The level of interest was refreshingly high; better still, I received a wholesale demand to learn the craft. There are now plans in place for me to carry out a series of training days, which will culminate in a hedgelaying competition. Competition is a bedrock of Young Farmers life, anything from tug-o-war to livestock judging; so is, for that matter, enjoying a beer or two afterwards. The YFC are obvious candidates to focus on, because the organisation already has at its heart the twin ideologies of sustainable farming and a wildlife-rich countryside. Members, whether working on their own farms, for others, or still at school, are superbly placed to begin managing hedges in their own *terroir*. Best still, there is no finer thing than seeing day after day the hedges you have worked on regrow and become filled with life, all thanks to your own efforts. It makes the tough job of farming that bit better.

The next candidate for our hedgers of tomorrow are ecology students. There are 5,000 qualified ecologists in Britain and over 400,000 working within the sector. Many work in or around farmland, which makes up over 70 per cent of the British landmass. As a result, most are more than aware of the challenges to nature caused by agriculture as well as by housebuilding, infrastructure projects, road building, increased levels of public access and road traffic. Whatever negative experiences I may have had with the woeful water-company ecologists, most doubtless enter the profession because they want to do good and bear a passion for the natural world. However, with such a wealth of numbers already working in the sector, newly qualified graduates say they struggle to find roles, pleading the chief hurdle is the supply of talent far outweighing demand. It seems ludicrous, then, that these young and clearly engaged people are not encouraged to look at more hands-on work in conservation as an option after they leave university, either as a medium-term measure or as a long-term career. More ridiculous yet is that there is so little opportunity for these young people to train in the skills required, should they choose the less academic and more practical path – be that hedgelaying, arboriculture, coppicing or of course agriculture itself. A criticism many ecologists receive from farmers is that they have a lot of theory and too little practical skill. The Chartered Institute of Ecology and Environmental Management (CIEEM) are not blind to this accusation and revealed in a 2019 report, written by the institute's education and professional development officer, Nick Jackson, 'There is currently a major concern within the sector that a skills gap has arisen and is widening.' He adds, 'Field/practical skills are essential for entering the profession. These practical skills are rarely gained through university courses.' Despite the clear issue of oversupply, thirty-seven UK universities continue to offer eighty-one degree courses in ecology.

Learning how to lay a hedge is admittedly a struggle, particularly if you are not from a rural area or have few connections with the agricultural community. This shortage of practical education has been compounded by the number of agricultural colleges, now more commonly known as 'land-based colleges', declining by 80 per cent in the past four decades, according to a 2022 published report by an all-party Defra committee. A few remaining land-based colleges, such as Kingston Maurward in Dorset, offer hedgelaying training, amounting to a few hours of practical and theoretical experience, as part of certificate courses in countryside management. Others, like the College of Agriculture, Food and Rural Enterprise (CAFRE) in Northern Ireland, provide day-release training in hedgelaying for those already working in game management, agriculture or arboriculture. A number of professional hedgelayers offer training courses privately for anyone with an interest in the craft; this is something Gouldy and I cannot do, simply because we are too busy laying hedges for farmers. Even taking on an apprentice is challenging. First, professional hedgelayers have no access to the government's funding for apprenticeship providers; the closest would be either arboriculture or fencing! Equally our work is seasonal; I would have to pay an apprentice for five summer months of inactivity, which would be good neither for the apprentice nor for my already delicate bank balance. In Essex a five-month full-time hedgelaying traineeship was put on offer for the 2024 hedging season. This was funded by CPRE, with the successful candidate receiving full training from a professional hedgelayer, resulting in a LANTRA bronze award in competency and a safe-chainsaw-handling certificate. This is an excellent idea, arguably a benchmark for a future training model that could and should be funded by central government. It is clearly unsustainable to rely upon a charity to fund an entire nationwide training programme for hedgelayers.

The cause of this skills shortage appears to be largely the lack of communication between government departments. It also highlights the persistent indifference, by the wider body politic, to real-world challenges of taking political, environmental and agricultural aspirations and putting them into practice. Even before the UK voted to leave the EU, farming was clearly on the cusp of another agricultural revolution, with a clear move away from maximum production to a more sustainable and environmentally focused model. Post-Brexit, the announcement of the end of BPS and the arrival of ELMs underlined this fact. It was obvious that, for farmers to provide these 'public goods for public money', a range of new skills, or more accurately, forgotten and ignored skills, would need to be relearned by the rural workforce. Sadly, the education ministry seemed to be oblivious to any skills shortage. They failed to heed the 70 per cent shortfall in arboricultural staff as highlighted to them by the Institute of Chartered Foresters, meaning woods would not be planted, coppiced or managed. They ignored calls from the NFU that the agricultural workforce was nearly 50 per cent understaffed. They failed to see that nearly 500,000 kilometres of hedgerows would need more than a few rum old boys from Suffolk to manage them.

To Defra's credit, the department moved with remarkable speed to create a new national scheme for agricultural reform. Of course, this process was filled with complications. These were, at the macro level, caused by diversity of soils, variance in farming systems and market forces; at the micro level, factors such as tradition and reluctance to change contributed to a febrile atmosphere among individual farmers, industry leaders and an assortment of wildlife charities, all of whom believed their voices were ignored during the development stage. The referee for this rural bunfight was and continues to be Janet Hughes, Defra's director of farming reforms. It is rare for a civil servant to be seen as a heroine, yet this is what Janet became. Aware that the countryside sees change as a thing to be avoided, she travelled the country with an evangelistic zeal, universally winning friends along the way. She visited individual farmers, farm clusters, nature reserves and public meetings in village halls, and even cajoled assorted rustics to join steering groups via Zoom. She facilitated the airing of opinions and the forming of a consensus; this became a truly democratic process, a rare thing indeed. I became part of her hedgerows and boundaries steering group. I sat through hours of online meetings, contributing, listening, learning about the huge variation in requirements and management practices our hedges demand from Cornwall to Cumbria, Suffolk to Shropshire. The result, wholly thanks to Janet's dynamism, pragmatism and ability to listen, is that our hedgerows are now better protected and better funded than at any time in our agricultural history. If there is one person who should be honoured as the true hero of the English hedge, it is not a hedgelayer, a naturalist, an ecologist, a campaigner or a politician. It is a civil servant called Janet; our farmland wildlife owes her much. If all of that work and consensus-building is derailed because we lack the human resource to carry it out, then our politicians have failed. Nature's decline is solely down to them.

Learning to be a hedgelayer is not as simple as it should be.

This is a pity. It is clear there is a pressing need for more of our tribe, be they independent contractors, such as Gouldy and me, or agricultural workers, who include the craft in their portfolio of skills. The funding mechanisms for better management of hedgerows are now fully in place through ELMs and Countryside Stewardship; their protection is enshrined in law under the Management of Hedgerows (England) Regulations 2024. Their role as habitats, food providers and corridors for wildlife is fully understood by conservationists. Meanwhile, the hedgerow's wider environmental benefits, as a filtration system ensuring cleaner water, as carbon store, or in flood prevention, are still being studied by scientists. Without doubt the hedgerow continues to retain its original agricultural purpose, supporting our food production systems by sheltering livestock, preventing soil erosion and giving protection to growing crops. The wider public, too, adores the hedge. Poetry is written in its honour. Jams, drinks and pies are made from its fruits. Or it is simply appreciated, loved even, for its bucolic beauty, seen as a quintessential part of the English lowland landscape. It is curious, perhaps, that we have all grown to love our hedgerows. Not so long ago they were overlooked, a part of the countryside that came and went like a tide; borne on the vagaries of the rural economy and farming practice.

I have written this book for everyone who loves our hedgerows. Within these pages I have tried to express my words from the hedge. Some may find my views on shooting, gamekeepers, deer- and predator-control controversial; a few may find them unpalatable. I make no apology for this. The English countryside is a living thing, a beautiful thing, and it is a workplace, my workplace, and every inch of it has been wholly moulded by humans. We have made the English landscape; nothing remains 'wild' in the true sense of the word. The hedge is the epitome of this statement. No hedge is wild, each one was planted by human hand. If we walk away from them, they cease to be hedgerows, either failing, or turning into a distinctly poorer habitat. It is my privilege to work in the hedge, and I hope that these words inspire others to learn the craft of hedgelaying, be that with formality and regard for tradition as a competition layer, or in a conservation style that is wholly done for wildlife. And even if you have no wish to pick up a billhook or wield a chainsaw, I hope *Words from the Hedge* inspires you to look deeper into these leafy lines of shrubby thorn, barb and flower. For in here are true wonders. The hedgerow is the very best of us.

Conservation hedgelaying and how you can do it

Part of the inspiration for writing this book was about wanting more people to lay hedges, be it in your garden, on some land owned by a local farmer, or even on land of your own. The easiest method and the best method for wildlife is, as you probably know I'm about to say, conservation laying.

Conservation hedgelaying is inarguably the most efficient method of laying and rejuvenating hedges. It is particularly effective on hedgerows that have been planted in the past twenty years under stewardship grants or on older hedges that have been coppiced in the past decade. On previously coppiced hedgerows this conservation style lays the multi-stemmed regrowth, creating a thicker base than that achieved by coppicing alone. Side growth is removed, particularly any limbs and brash that face downwards on the laid pleacher. Brush on the top of the limb and growth that faces upwards are largely left in place, unless this interferes with 'building the hedge'. In this circumstance the brush can either be laid into the hedge or removed. Pleachers are laid low between thirty and forty degrees in the direction of uphill, cut using either a chainsaw or billhook in a slanted downwards manner so that a hinge is created. They can either be staked or, if plentiful limbs are available, living stakes are created by pollarding one stem every metre or so, into which the pleachers are woven. Heels are finished off cleanly with a diagonal downwards cut. No binding is necessary, but brush can be tidied with billhook or chainsaw to ensure that the finished hedge is thick and wind-rock resistant. The finished hedge should be at a height of between 3 ft 6 in to 4 ft (1 m to 1.2 m), but this is somewhat dependent on the hedge you are working on.

Some favoured plants for an East Anglian hedge

Field Maple

A small- to medium-sized tree. Prone to dominance in strong clay or drier soils. The small yellow-green flowers, essential for early pollinators, appear in April. The field maple is favoured by many aphid species, which in turn attract hugely beneficial predatory insects such as ladybird and hoverfly. It was said hanging a field maple branch outside your front door kept bats out.

Common Dogwood

A true dense-hedgerow shrub. The shade tolerance it shows is useful for planting under hedgerow trees, as is its ability to grow in extremes of wet or dry. In May the unpleasant-smelling clusters of white flowers attract pollinators, and the berries that turn to black in autumn are a staple for many farmland birds and mammals. Dogwood twigs were traditionally used as meat skewers by butchers. The cross of Christ was allegedly crafted from dogwood.

Hazel

Naturally forming a multi-stemmed bush, the hazel is the greatest ally to coppicers and hedgelayers. It grows well in most soils and is best planted well spaced out along a hedge. Hazel is monoecious. Its male flowers, yellow catkins, appear in mid-February before the leaves, the female flowers look like red buds. Once pollinated by the wind, the female flowers form into a clump of three of four fruits that mature to become nuts. One of the many hazel uses was in water divining. This technique for finding springs and forgotten waterpipes in fields is still in use today. Personally, I use two wire coat hangers.

Hawthorn

The king of the East Anglian hedge, the hawthorn is a thorny shrub that will, if permitted, grow into a gnarled tree. The lobed leaves emerge coloured a citrus green, darkening as they mature. Its famed May blossom is made up of tiny clusters of sweet-smelling flowers that are a boon to many pollinators. As the blossom fades, they become bunches of attractive berries which are eaten by an array of birds and mammals. In new hedgerow plantations, hawthorn generally makes up 70 per cent of the species. Traditionally the hawthorn made the crown for the Green Man. It is said to bring bad luck if hawthorn flowers are brought into the house – they certainly do bring with them a plentiful supply of small flea beetles that will infest your windowsill.

Spindle

In strong East Anglian soil, the spindle belies its reputation for slow growth, swiftly becoming a somewhat leggy addition to a hedge. The nondescript lemon-coloured flowers erupt in May and June; by autumn they turn into gaudy pink berries that open to reveal four yellow seeds within. The leaves are essential food for magpie, spindle ermine and scorched wing moths. Dunnock seem to particularly adore the gaudy fruits. Although both fruit and leaves are toxic to humans, spindle was prized for its traditional uses including the manufacture of wool spindles, gunpowder and artist's charcoal.

Holly

Every plant has its place, and in the hedge the holly's is under the shade of trees. Achingly slow to grow, the glossy evergreen leaves are inhospitably sharp towards the base, becoming more oval further up the tree where they are no longer prone to being browsed by deer and hares. Small white flowers, once pollinated, become the well-known scarlet berries so beloved of wreath-makers along with birds such as redwings and fieldfares fresh in from migration. The Christmas tradition of bringing holly into the house stems from a pagan ritual where evil spirits would be caught in the spiky leaves of a holly bough hung over the door.

Sea Buckthorn

Commonly found, as the name indicates, in coastal areas, particularly along the Sandlings of Suffolk. The long, thin, silvery leaves shine green-grey in a sea breeze. The highly perfumed pastel-orange fruits of autumn are formed from undramatic flowers that bloom in late April. The spikes on the branches of sea buckthorn are hideously sharp. The winter migrant, the great grey shrike, uses these for a gibbet on which to store prey, including beetles, small reptiles and birds. Sea buckthorn was supposedly the favoured food of the winged horse Pegasus.

Purging Buckthorn

Glossy, dark green leaves turn a dramatic yellow in autumn. Buckthorn is picky about soil, seeming to fail in the finest arable varieties. Tiny greeny-yellow flowers, both male and female, appear in late spring. Once pollinated, the females produce shiny black berries which are important food sources for many farmland bird species. Buckthorn leaves are essential food for the caterpillars of the brimstone butterfly. The plant gains its name from its purgative properties; it is also an irritant and appears to be the cause of my persistent psoriasis.

Crab Apple

Whether the crabs we find dotted in nearly every hedgerow are truly wild varieties, or trees that have grown as a result of a ploughman discarding an apple core, is a work of study for a botanist not a hedger. Whatever the truth, the blossom that blooms from late April to mid-May is a boon for pollinators, and the fruits are adored by many birds, thrushes and blackbirds in particular. You can lay a crab, but we tend to leave them as hedgerow trees. It is said that if you throw crab apple pips in the fire and they explode, then your love is true.

Blackthorn

Along with the hawthorn, the blackthorn is the staple hedgerow shrub. Hardy and capable of growing in any soil, the blackthorn suckers readily. Whilst this is no problem in livestock hedges, it can swiftly become an invasive troublemaker in arable settings of hedgerows and margins. The thorns are savage and covered in a verdigris-like 'must' that causes infections in human hands, dogs' knees or horses' legs. Blackthorn blossom is similar to that seen on hawthorn, but appears a month or so earlier, in March. The fruits, known as sloes, are astringent and bitter to human tastes (unless mixed with gin, sugar and a drop or two of vanilla essence). Farmland birds have no such qualms. Blackthorn is popular with ravenous birds in winter, particularly after a frost, when the sloes lose their matt appearance and begin to soften. A plant associated with sinister ill omens, the modern English word 'strife' is thought to be rooted in the old Celtic word for blackthorn, *straif*.

Guelder Rose

The only non-native species in this list, the guelder adores all East Anglian soils, particularly those that have chalk in their makeup. Shade-tolerant, and vigorous once established, guelder rose thrives with its roots in a wet ditch. The leaves are similar to a maple's and the broad clusters of white flowers that become tightly packed at the centre are fragrant and popular with a host of small pollinators and beneficial predatory insects, particularly hoverflies. The clusters of waxy red berries that form are popular with many farmland birds, and the shrub's speedy and dense reaction to either laying or coppicing make for an excellent conservation-focused hedge. There is no British folklore associated with the non-native guelder rose; it is, however, one of the national symbols of Ukraine.

A Note on Sources

For those keen to learn more about the craft, history and theory of hedgelaying and hedgerow management, I highly recommend reading *Hedges and Hedgelaying* by Murray Maclean, published by The Crowood Press Ltd. The symbiosis of farming and game management are best understood through reading a duo of out-of-print books in tandem: firstly, *Memoirs of a Gamekeeper* by Tom Turner (published by Geoffrey Bles), and then *The Elveden Enterprise: A Story of the Second Agricultural Revolution* by George Martelli (Faber & Faber Ltd). The fascinating *Medieval Suffolk: An Economic and Social History 1200–1500* by Mark Bailey (Boydell Press) is essential reading to better understand the long-standing dominance of agriculture in East Anglia. Studying any of the works by the peerless Henry Williamson is time well spent, but his *Story of a Norfolk Farm* (reissued by Clive Holloway Books) gives particular insight to farming and the countryside in the 1930s and early war years; and to the troubled mind of one of Britain's greatest ever nature writers. *The Fens* by Francis Pryor (Bloomsbury) weaves archaeology, history and peat soil into a fascinatingly grubby whole, perfect reading for those interested in the 'rum old place' that is fenland. A visit to the museum and gallery at Gainsborough's House in Sudbury enables you to time-travel and experience the Georgian boom years of farming in Suffolk. Likewise, an afternoon spent in the National Gallery viewing

'Honest John' Constable's paintings discloses both the beauty and stark reality of East Anglia in times of agricultural depression. Finally, I recommend taking out a subscription to the online magazine *Scribehound* (www.scribehound.com). My fellow contributors include Roger Morgan-Grenville, Patrick Laurie, Jamie Blackett, Claire Taylor, Owen Williams and Anna Jones, all providing an expert and truly balanced view of modern farming, land management and conservation. The integrity and practicality you find in their words are a rare phenomenon, a counterpoint to those authors and journalists who use and abuse the countryside and its people to promote an unwanted culture war – a war that does nothing but harm our precious British wildlife.

Acknowledgements

I firstly thank my wife, Clare, for putting up with the filth, sawdust, blood and sweat – you are indeed my world. Much love to my son, Charlie – what a grand young man you are. The main reason *Words from the Hedge* ever made it from my head to the page is due to my friend Patrick Galbraith – you have been a supportive rock and a superb editor. My cap is raised to John Mitchinson at Unbound, who took a risk on me. Emotionally, I lean heavily on my dogs – what a debt I owe Mabel and Blyth, who keep me sane, as does Richard Gould, the finest of men and most trusted of pals. To my unflappably swan-like agent Emma Shercliff, who laughs at most of my jokes – you deserve every glass of champagne you are offered. My wholehearted admiration and gratitude go to Flo at Unbound and Mary Chesshyre, who tamed this straggly, overgrown hedge of a book and turned it into something more biodiverse and manageable; so, too, Becca Thorne, who turned my words into pictures. Heartfelt thanks go to Cedric Burton, Jonathan Minter, Squire Gerald de Lisle and Robert Graves, a quartet of grand old countrymen and mentors. To all of the farmers I work for, I extend not only my thanks but my regard: you have one of the hardest jobs in the world and receive little to no thanks for your efforts, particularly from those with comfortably full bellies: special mention to Jeremy Squirrel, Ed Nesling, Martin Stuffins, Squeak Denny, Tom Martin, Sam Carlisle, Charles Shropshire,

Tom Jewers, Jim Allen, Roger and Adam Steed, the Barker family and James Black. My parents, Dorothy and David Negus, deserve special mention; they taught me much. To Deadly Darren Sizer: you are a prince among men, so too are my journalistic sidekick Callum, and my Northern correspondents Dave and Graham, thank you all for the endless laughter. The teams at the GWCT, the Suffolk Agricultural Association, Scribehound, and Mark and Eliza at Operation Turtle Dove – you are all heroes in your own ways. To my pals the Garners, I raise a glass and my bat to Ross and my teammates at Eye and District Cricket Club, without whom summers would be dull. Likewise, I lift my barrels to my fellow Great Yarmouth Wildfowlers, who make my fleeting periods of free time in winter exciting. I will inevitably have forgotten to mention many supportive friends and colleagues, to whom I excuse myself by blaming it all on advancing age and an increasing level of chainsaw-induced tinnitus for their absence from this list. Finally, I would like to thank three men who are no longer with us in body, but their spirit lives on through my work: Joe Rowntree, Tony Butler and Michael Dixon – you will never be forgotten, the countryside lay safe in your hands and it is my duty to continue your gentle legacy.

Unbound is a publisher which champions bold, unexpected books.

We give readers the opportunity to support books directly, so our authors are empowered to take creative risks and write the books they really want to write. We help readers to discover new writing they won't find anywhere else.

We are building a community in which authors engage directly with people who love what they do. It's a place where readers and writers can connect with and support one another, enjoy unique experiences and benefits, and make books that matter.

This book is in your hands because readers made it possible. Everyone who pledged their support is listed below. Join them by visiting unbound.com and supporting a book today.

K. Aagard
Drew Adams
John Adams
Edward Aldus
Kelly Allen
Margaret Ambrose
Jane Angell
Benjamin NH Aplin
Jacqueline Arasi
Nick Armstrong
Tamara Arntzen
Colin Arthurs
Sabrina Artus
Kate Ashley
Robert Ashton
Aoife and Esme Austen
James Aylett

Justin B
Nat Bacon
Constance Meath Baker
Elizabeth Meath Baker
Tim Baldwin
John Barber
Claire Barker
Matthew Barrett
Naomi Barrow
Stephen Bartlett
Neil Barton
Gergely Battha-Pajor
Andrew Batty
Guy Baxendale
Emma Bayliss
Ron Baynes

Ed Bedford
Shahin Bekhradnia
Gertie Bell
Edward Bennett
Daisy Benson
Steve Besley
Hannah Best
Melanie Bhavsar
Robin Bickley
Pauline Biron
Helen Blamires
Michael Blanche
Graham Blenkin
Sean Bloomsburg
Justin Bonnet
Jacqueline Boston
Colin & Jenny Boswell

SUPPORTERS

Philip Breen
Orlando Bridgeman
Elizabeth Briggs
Ashley Bristowe
Simon Broad
Antonia Brotchie
Rebecca Brouwers-
    Harries
Deborah Brower
Andy Brown
George Browne
Ewan Buckingham
Guy Buckingham
Karl Bull
Mike Bull
Jeremy Burchardt
Simon Burdett
Laurette Burton
Mark Butler
Tom Byers
Susan Byrne
Kevin Callahan
Matt Callow
Darren Cameron
Elizabeth Card
Dr Darren Richard
    Carlaw
Sam Carlisle
Robert Carnes
John Carrick
Rowena Case
Phil Champion
Vicki Chapman
Jo Chopra-
    McGowan
Ford Chris
Mary Christian
Simon Clark
Chris Claxton
Mathew Clayton
Andrew Coates
Virginia Coe

Caroline Colgan
Wendy Connor
Dan Connors
Alexander Cooper
Jamie Cooper
Paul Counter
Thomas Coutts
Bill Cox
Nancy Crosby
Alasdair Cross
N. Crotty
Miranda Cuming
Lesley Cundy
Janet Cunningham
Pamela Cunningham
Kath Curran-White
S D
Jane and Breezy
    Dallaway
Dameon
Antoine Darbois
Lauren Davidson &
    Wayland Gill
Cathy Davies
Meryl Davies
Nigel Davies
Richard Davies
Roslyn Davies
Ian Davis
Laura Davis
Clara Decerbo
Colin Dente
Daisy dePaulis
Liz Dexter
Rachel Dixon
Hazel Douglas
Roger Draycott
Charlie Drew
Jacob Duellman
Jane Dunster
Eastern Counties
    Mink Hunt

Emma & William
    Ede-Smith
Paul Edwards
Perryn Edwards
Marti Eller
Mark Elliott
Tom Elliott
Susanne Emde
Christopher Everest
Sheila Ewers
Louise Farmer
Julia Feakes
Felix Cobbold Trust
Lydia Ferguson
Richard Ferguson
Sarah Ferguson
Simon Filbrun
Cheryl Finlay
Cathy Fisher
Jeff Foreman
Chris Fosten
Jacques Francis
Bob Freshwater
Robert Frewen
Kevin Froud
Stephen Furlong
Deborah Gage
Patrick Galbraith
Max Gallagher
Chris Gamble
Mark Gamble
Mary Garland
Nick, Mary, Eleanor,
    Charlotte and
    Georgina Garner
Wendy Garrigus
Julie Giles
Juliana Glanfield
James Goodman
Justin Grady
Graeme
Kyle Graham

Al Green
Col Green
Jon Green
Marcus Green
Marion Greene
Keith Gregory
Linda Gregory
Felix Griffin
Mike Griffiths
Claire Grinham
Mathew Grove
Andy Gunton
Kay Haggie
Chris Haigh
J Haigh
Kate Hall
Laurence Hall
Scott Hamilton
Jack Hammond
Jeremy Hanks
Gerri Hanus
Edward Hardwick
Richard Hardy
Robin Hargreaves
Johanna Harman
Johnathan Harpham
Amanda and Martin Harrison
Elaine Hathaway
Susie Hawkes
Paul Haynes
Christine Healey
Sheila Hedges
Kit Henson
Charles Herbert
Kimberly Hickman
Matt Higgs
Charlotte Hignett
Brendon Hill
Kirk Hill
Catherine Hills
William Hite
Cheryl Hobson
Kathryn Hodgson
Marie Hodgson
Jay Hohl
Pamela Holm
Henry Hopking
Jason Hopper
Philip Hoskin
Philippa Hoskin
Tom Hostler
Jackie Howard-Birt
Roger Huggett
Kieran Hughes
Patricia Hughes
Julie Humphreys
Ian F Hunter
Jeff Hunter
Sophie Ibbotson
Shaun Irving
Charlie Irwin
Oliver Ivory-Bray
Paul Jabore
Philip Jackson
Mike James
Toby Jeffries
Paul Johnson
Mark Johnstone
Nigel Joice
Ross Jolliffe
Johnny Jones
Tony Jones
Matt Joye
Mike Jury
Sue Jury
Lizzie Kathiravel
Imogen Kelly
S. G. Kelly
James Kennedy
Jo Kennedy
Mary Kersey
Rebecca Kershaw
Martin Killick
Ingrid Kincaid
Janet King
Angela Kingman
David Kinnersley
Brian Kirkbride
Jackie Kirkham
Aarni Koskela
Emily Kyne
Gabrielle Laine-Peters
Naomi Langford-Wood
Nigel Larke
James Larner
Tom Law
Robbie Lawler
Brian Lawley
Andy Lawrence
Oscar Leach
Richard Leach
Sam Lee
Justin Leighton
Andrew Lewis
Kirsty Lewis
Simon Lindsley
Toby Lingard
Carole Lis
Sam Lord
Love, Daisy & Clarke
Ben Lovelady
Raymond Lowell
Alan Lowey
Kieron Lyons
Lee Mabbutt
Adrian Mabe
Dan Madden
Samuel Mahoney
Ben Makowiecki
Nigel Manning
Kate Maple
Aron Markey
Sarah Marshall

Adam Martin
Tom Martin
Ian Masterton
Duncan Mathieson
Susan Matthews
Kyle McAbee
In loving memory of Carol McConnell
Stephen McGinn
Penny McGregor
Stewart Mcintyre
Brian Mcmillan
Calum McRoberts
Jennie Mead
Rod Mearing
Michael Messham
Marc Metzger
Johan Meylaerts
Kizzia Mildmay
Belle Miles
Andrew Millar
Judith Miller
Natalie Milne
John Mitchinson
Jonathan Moore
Alison Mormino
Gillian Mortimer
Tommy Morton
Kim Mullen-Kuehl
Barbara Murray
Robert Naylor
Charlie Negus
Clare Negus
David Negus
David & Dorothy Negus
Antony Nelson
Bridget Newbery
Jack Nice
Rosie Nicol-Harper
Niels Aagaard Nielsen
Robert Nix

Steven Noel
Emily Nolan
Tony Norman
Christine Norrie
Conrad Norris
Mark Nowers
Shelagh O'Riordan
David O'Reilly
Angela Osborne
Sian Owen
Stuart Packington
Paula Page
Hanne Gates Paine & John Daniels
Aggy Palairet
Peter Parker
Richard Parker
Adam Parmenter
Ian Lloyd Parry
Claire Parsons
Sue Patrick
Donald Patterson
Christine Pawlica
Gavin Peacock
Sophie Peckham
Robin Pembrooke
John Pendleton
Richard Penney
Sarah Perrett
Anne Pettifor
James Petts
Jakki Phillips
Jonathan Phillips
Jonathan Philp
Wendy Pickering
Chip Pitfield
Kristin Plant
Louise Pollard
Carla Pont
David Poole
Gemma Porch
Rebecca Powell

Sebastian Powell
Chris Pribe
Richard Prideaux
Stephen Priestley
Rebecca Rajendra
James Ramskir-Gardiner
Kathleen Read
Paul Read
James Reed
David Rees
Alistair Renwick
Timothy Rhinehart
John Richardson
Shaun Riordan
RJCKB
Carl Roberts
Magz Roberts
Austin Robinson
James Rose
Rosewood Farm
Melanie Rosenthal
Gary Ross
Richard Rout
Rachel Rowe
Billy Rowland
Joe Rowntree
Yvonne Rowse
Alistair Rush
Janet Rutter
Sean Ryan
Sean Ryan
Nicholas Peter Savage
Perry Sawyer
Janette Schubert
Anne-Marie Scott
Manda Scott
Mark Scott
Philip Scott
Tom Scott
Chris Self
Heather Self

Karen Selley
Dick Selwood
Ami Shah
Gloria Shaw
Dearbhla Sheridan
Katherine Sherwin
Ewan Shilland
James Shipman
Alison Shore
Michael Short
Nick Short
Ruth Singer
Tony Sinnott
Angelika Smith
Colin and Helen Smith
David Smith
Gavin Smith
Harvey Smith
Scott Smith
Benjamin Somner-Bogard
Jo Spillane
Leigh Spilsbury
Tania Spooner
Eugenia Sproul
Teresa Squires
Jeremy Squirrell
Hetty Startup
Michael Stephenson | Rodney Corrigan
Hamish Stewart
Mandy Stokes
Aurora Stone
Gisela Stuart
Andrew Sunnucks
Nigel Swann
Robert Swann
Vanessa Swetman
Andreas Tack
Phillip Tailby
Eve Tallis
Jayne Tansey-Patron
Sarah Tasker
Kathryn Taylor
Paul Taylor
Emily Terry
Emma Thimbleby
Richard Thomas
Brewer Thompson
David Thompson
Helen Thompson
Liz Thompson
J Thrupp
Adam Tinworth
Sybil Lark James Todd
William Tremlett
Lou Turnbull
Nigel Vardy
Sandy Vaughan
Sarah Vaughan
William Vaughan
Rebecca Vaughn
Andrew Vermes
Roger Viggers
Percy Vogel
Victoria von Biel
Nienke Vos
Bill Wadsworth
Anne Waldon
Mark Walker
Sarah Walker
Robert Wallis
Carole-Ann Warburton
Richard Warnes
Michael Watson
Tamsin Watts
Christopher Webb
E Webb
Sam Webley
Oliver Wells
Travis West
Paul Shildon White
Gary Stuart Wicks
Heather Wiggin
Linda Wike
Barry Wilkes
Gareth Williams
Pete Williams
Sarah Windrum
Magi Winmillhermann
Lorna Wolf
Lucy Wood
John Woodmansey
Heather Woods
Peter Woolley
Veronica Worrall
Adam Wright
Cassidy Wright
Liam Wylie
Rob Wylie
Yvonne Yelland
Angharad Yeo
Debbie Young
Peter Zacharias
Sally Zaranko
Graham Zimmermann

A Note on the Author

Richard Negus is a former soldier and professional horseman. He now lays hedges for a living and is an award-winning conservationist. He lives in rural Mid Suffolk with his wife Clare, his son Charlie and their gundogs Mabel and Blyth. His writing champions the people, wildlife and landscape of his native Suffolk countryside and his work can be found in publications including *Scribehound, Country Life* and *The Critic*.

A Note on the Type

The text of this book is set in Adobe Garamond Pro. Released in 1989, it is a digital adaptation of the roman types of Claude Garamond and the italic types of Robert Granjon. It's one of several versions of Garamond. It is believed that Garamond based his font on Bembo, cut in 1495 by Francesco Griffo in collaboration with the Italian printer Aldus Manutuis. Garamond types were first used in printed books in Paris around 1532.